GRACE

GRACE

JOHN R BRODERICK

XULON PRESS

Xulon Press
2301 Lucien Way #415
Maitland, FL 32751
407.339.4217
www.xulonpress.com

Printed in the United States of America

Paperback ISBN-13: 978-1-66281-622-2
Ebook ISBN-13: 978-1-66281-623-9

ACKNOWLEDGMENTS

I'VE HAD CHURCH PEOPLE SAY TO ME, "JOHN, TELL God your plans, and He'll laugh at you." I had never planned to write this book. I am now middle-aged at sixty years old, and I would not have had this God-altering-life event happen if it were not for the "Fall." It has been a blessing to me to type this entire book not on my normal pre-dominantly right side, but with one finger on my left hand, confined to a wheelchair with four fractured ribs and my left eye closed due to severe double vision. I want to first acknowledge and thank the responding EMTs, all the doctors, nurses, nurse's aides, and the chaplains at Boston Medical Center for saving my life. I want to thank the entire staff at Spaulding Rehab Hospital in Charlestown, Massachusetts, where my recovery journey first began and continues to this day. Special thanks to my physical therapist Dr. Abbey and occupational therapist Alana, who started it all. To Bob O'Donnell, thank you for all you have done interacting with Claire and my family. You were there for them when I was first transported to Boston Medical Center, and you continue to be an inspiration to us all.

A special thank-you to Pastor Mike Feehan, Arlene, and the congregation of Lighthouse Fellowship Church for their continuing prayers and financial blessings. Thank you for all the meals you all have unselfishly brought to my family. Deepest of gratitude to Mayor Thomas Koch and his wife Kristine, who have been a true Godsend to me and my family.

Also, a special thank-you to Helen and the Quincy Foundation for all their help. Thank you to the Quincy School Department and our North Quincy High School family. You have all been a true blessing not only to me but to our entire family as well.

Thank you to Pastor Aaron Cavin and Life Community Church for your continued spiritual and financial support. To my neighbor Tina Falconi, writer of children's books, thank you for your invaluable input on the cover work of the book.

To a lifelong friend and man of God, Chris Guin. Thank you for all the encouragement and invaluable work on the "GRACE" website.

Thank-you to Pastor Bill Donahue and wife Daisy Donahue for leading me to the Christ in 1997 at the Lords Planting Church in Quincy, Massachusetts. You have both been a blessing being there for Claire and myself both in the good times and times of hardship.

I will be eternally grateful to the late John Baker, his wife Cheryl, and Pastor Rick Warren for the ministry of Celebrate Recovery. It was a blessing to be a ministry leader for many years serving while helping others.

To Claire's sister Barbara, from the beginning your personal and emotional sacrifice has been immeasurable not only to me but to Claire and our children as well. To Karen, Claire's older sister, thank you for being the prayer warrior you have always been, especially in this most difficult time for us all.

Brothers and Sisters in Christ and all who have prayed for me, many of whom I don't know, thank you. I believe without a doubt it is because of all of you that I am here.

Finally, to my wife Claire , twenty-eight years married, there are no words to express my all-encompassing love and deep gratitude I have for you. No one should ever have to carry all the pain, suffering and fears of uncertainty as you have. Yet you did it with faithfulness, compassion, and a persevering Spirit to this day. Claire, you are living out the truth of our wedding vows, "For better or for worse, in sickness or in health." You have been a true Godsend.

Since that fateful Sunday in January of 2020, almighty God has shown me just how blessed I am to have the three beautiful children I have. Britney, twenty-six, Brianna, twenty, and

Robert, eighteen years old. Three children, whom I adore with all that I am and only wish I could hug them every day, but for now I am physically unable to.

Lord God of all creation, at first, I did not understand why this had happened to me and why you would have allowed it. I thought I was serving you on Christian radio and in Christian recovery. I have been guilty of having a classic pity party for myself, and for that I ask for your forgiveness, Lord. I see clearly and without a doubt that I am to glorify you, Lord, and you will be better served in my current condition for now. This is my purpose. I know that it will not be easy. I come humbly before you and praying for continued strength for myself, Claire, and our family, oh God. May these true-life examples and writings be pleasing to you, your Son, my Lord Jesus Christ, and the Holy Spirit. Thank you, Lord, for providing a permanent home for my mother-in-law, Barbara Hewitt Sr., who believes in you, oh God. The doctors said that her journey here on earth would be over in just a few short hours from the completion of this book. Thank you for your promise of Heaven, Lord. Amen.

> **25 Jesus said to her, "I am the resurrection and the life. The one who believes in me will live, even though they die;" NIV.**

Love,
John Broderick

TABLE OF CONTENTS

NOTE FROM THE AUTHOR

THE END OF CHAPTER 1, **"THE FALL,"** AND THE
very next chapter **"FROZEN"** through Chapter 9, **"MISTAKEN
IDENTITY"** are all true stories that happened to me as an
older teenager and into my young adulthood. These incidents
occurred well before I knew who God really was.

My late mom Andria, being from Rome, Italy, raised all 4
of us children as Roman Catholics as best she could. It wasn't
until I was thirty-seven years old, the summer of **1997** that I
received Jesus Christ as my Lord and Savior and began to start
a personal relationship with Him. It wasn't until just after the
"Fall" in 2020, at the age of **fifty-nine**, that the Lord my God
began to **clearly** reveal His Righteousness and undying love for
me. To Glorify God is my only purpose for writing this book.

It may be somewhat confusing to some readers, and my
hope and prayer is that this **note**, would bring you greater
clarity and a better understanding of **"Grace."**

PROLOGUE

On January 5th, of 2020, time stood still. Having fallen down fourteen stairs, lying unconscious and bleeding from the mouth is how EMTs found me. Quincy Police and Fire showed up quickly, and my seventeen-year-old son Robert witnessed the entire fall. My wife, Claire, and daughter Britney rushed to the scene of flashing lights only minutes away. Through the many prayers of my family, friends, and people unknown, I am here.

This is my story.

THE FALL

I SAW ON TELEVISION THAT 2018 HAD BEEN ONE OF the hottest years on record. I must admit, I like the cool temperatures and winter a whole lot more. We had just finished up another enjoyable season of baseball watching my son Robert and North Quincy High School play. Claire, Britney, and I, along with Butterball, our beautiful and precious Golden Retriever, loved going to watch his games. She would be very content just lying in the grass and soaking up the sun as we all sat in our folding chairs with a bottle of water. Butterball is a wonderful dog bringing us lots of love and great memories. My daughter Brianna was usually in work at the Newport Ave Stop and Shop only minutes away from the baseball field. She would attend whenever she wasn't working. When we weren't playing, Robert and I would practice anytime we could. Being a bridge builder and doing a lot of concrete work as a former member of Carpenters Local #33, I was a pretty strong guy. Having had multiple hernia surgeries over the years did slow me down a bit, though, and forced me to go on disability. I was still in surprisingly good health and playing sports most of my life as a young teen and adult had certainly paid off. Being a husband and father to two girls and a boy came with its natural balancing act, of course. I would hit pop-ups with a tennis racket and tennis ball about 100 feet in the air, working on Robert's defense and ability to track down fly balls. I would play catch with him throwing the ball hard at times working on his coordination. We did all of this in front of our house and in the street. We would stop anytime a car would come by. We would occasionally go to newly built Creedon field, which was literally five minutes from us to practice whenever we could. I would use a regular aluminum baseball bat and baseball hitting Robert ground balls and pop-ups. I was also trying to get my Christian Non-Profit Anew Ministries Christ Centered Recovery up and fully functional.

Being brought up Roman Catholic and going to church on Christmas, Easter, Holy Days of Obligation, and occasional funerals, I kind of knew who God was. It wasn't until the spring of 1997 that I received Jesus Christ as my personal Lord and Savior which began to change my perspective on who God really is. It was the most important and critical decision I had ever made. I was blessed enough to be broadcasting on Boston's number-one Christian radio station, WEZE 590 AM The Word for several years. I would use a portion of my disability check every month just to stay on the air. I tried, but just could not get enough people to financially support the ministry after three years. I never took a cent for myself and was blessed to help many and stay on the air for as long as I did, even though the need seemed endless.

It was a cool and sunny thirty-five-degree day that January 5, 2020, and we certainly hadn't had much of a winter so far. Robert and I were getting ready to help my brother Jimmy move from his Hancock Street apartment in Quincy. Jimmy asked me earlier in the week if I would help him move. Being my older brother by just under eleven months, of course I said yes. Jimmy's health was not the best either, having type two diabetes and ongoing problems with his eyesight. Other than his nighttime vision being challenging for him, he got around pretty well.

Personally, I like the colder weather, as I could never get used to the heat. I would sweat uncomfortably during the warm weather and especially during the summer months. I was a lot like that scene in *Frosty the Snowman* when he gets locked in the greenhouse. I melt in the heat. The night before I had asked my son, Robert, if he would mind helping me move his uncle Jimmy. He said, "Sure, Dad, no problem." One thing about Robert, he has never shied away from any type of hard work. It most certainly didn't hurt to any degree that he was getting to ride in his future vehicle. Although, it was my truck, a purple 2007 Dodge RAM 1500 Quad Cab pickup with chrome plated rims, we wanted to give Robert something to work toward. My wife and I figured that we would give it to him as a graduation present with some conditions attached. First, Robert was to graduate with around a 3.0 grade average or better, otherwise, he wouldn't get the truck. When he does go off to college or out of state, then he would at least be able to drive there on his own. That was our thinking anyway.

So, we headed out onto Hancock Street, which is the main road that runs down the center of Quincy from beginning to end. We drove about a quarter mile up onto Hancock Street and came to Jimmy's home. Neither one of us had been there before, so we went to the front door of the address Jimmy gave us. We hopped out and parked on Hancock Street, which is a busy main street. We went up to the unlocked front door, opened it up, and went inside with Robert following right behind me. I immediately looked up the stairs and looked at the walls and thought to myself, "How the heck do people move in and out with nothing to grab onto." I must admit the walls looked almost majestic as they stretched from floor to the ceiling. Being a Union Carpenter for just over eighteen years and working on my own home, I observe other homes a bit more than most people. I told Robert to wait down here until I find out how we are going to do this. I figured by waiting down at the bottom of the stairs, Robert could also keep an eye on the truck.

As I was going up the stairs, I noticed that the stairwell curved to the right at the top. I thought it was very unusual for a front door entryway. It was a lot like the interior angled and winding stairs that I have in our house going up to the third floor. I said in a loud voice as I was walking up the stairs, "Jimmy, I'm here," as I could hear him singing to himself. He said, "Oh, what's up, John?" as I stepped onto the top stair closest to his room. Jimmy only had a smaller room on the left and shared a kitchen and bathroom. I said to him, "Does all this have to go?" He said, "Yep. Start with the newspapers over there," pointing to his right. I said, "Ok." I picked up a bundle and realized it was light for me, so I said to my brother, "Put another one," as I cradled the papers. Both of my hands were tied up carrying the first pile, so he did. "Don't take too many more because there heavy," Jimmy said. "I won't," I said.

There are two large differences between my brother and I, and they are perception and strength. I built bridges and did a lot of concrete work while a member of Carpenters Local 33. I was used to carrying heavier than normal weight loads. I remember taking the newspapers as I was walking out of his room, and I looked down to the bottom of the stairwell and saw Robert there waiting for me. I took a step and my foot slid off the smaller tapered edge causing me to slip and stumble. I instinctively dropped the newspapers, at the same time looking for something to grab onto. Nothing was there so I tucked my chin in toward my chest, as I was taught in Judo class. I hit the top of my head off the wall to my right, went totally blank, and fell down the remaining fourteen stairs landing at the bottom unconscious and bleeding from the mouth. My seventeen-year son Robert witnessed the entire fall and ever since has been traumatized by it. My brother Jimmy came running out from the sounds of the fall and yelled out to Robert, "Call nine-one-one!" So, he did. Jimmy hurriedly came down the stairs and cradled and raised my head as I landed on my backside facing up.

He wanted to make sure that I would not choke on my own blood. It reminded him of his best friend Stevie when we were younger, who he saw go through the windshield of a car right in front of him during an accident in South Boston years ago. Like me blood was coming out of Stevie's mouth as Jimmy tried to help him. But, unfortunately, Stevie passed away shortly after the accident. The ambulance, fire truck and police came quickly. It was about 11:30 a.m. when the ambulance drivers both came into the front door and told Jimmy to step aside from holding my head. Their training kicked in as they evaluated and treated me on the spot.

Robert called mom at home, and she did not answer her phone because she was in the bathroom. Upset and crying, Robert then called Britney, who told Claire that I had fallen. Claire and Britany wanted the ambulance to wait until they got there, so they told Robert to ask the ambulance driver to wait. The ambulance driver said that they didn't know if they could. Claire ran out the door in a hurry along with Britney without her sneakers on. They got there within minutes. The police were in the background as Claire and Britney talked with Robert, who was in the passenger front seat of the ambulance. By all departments being there with their flashing lights on, police, fire, and ambulance, it looked really serious. It was.

My head was bandaged up and I was quickly put onto a stretcher and wheeled into the back of the ambulance. I was unconscious, with a neck brace on, and three E.M.T.'s were trying to control the bleeding from my mouth and keep me alive. When Claire and Britney got there, Claire wanted them to take me to Beth Israel Milton Hospital, because that's the hospital that had all my medical records. "Mrs. Broderick, you do not understand," the ambulance driver said. We are going to have to take him to Boston Medical Center because they are a level-one trauma hospital and better equipped to handle injuries like this. So, I was rushed to Boston Medical Center Hospital not only because it was the closest trauma center, but it was world renowned as well. They were known for treating patients with serious life-threatening injuries, such as mine. As soon as we got to Boston Medical Center, I was wheeled directly into the intensive care unit (ICU) to a waiting team of doctors.

FROZEN

Sometimes in life there is an event that sticks out in our memory, and it never seems to go away. This is one that meteorologists will never forget. The day started out around a balmy thirty-eight degrees and would plummet down to the single digits at night. I had just got my license, and as a young teenager you could say that I felt invincible behind the wheel. I remember waking up to all the fresh snow outside my window and seeing how postcard picturesque it was. Snow always looks beautiful and pretty in its naturally fallen state. Little did I know what would unfold later that day during that massive historic storm. My mom had just told all four of us kids that her work had just called and asked her to come in. She told us that her supervisor said that there was a State of Emergency in Boston and that all essential workers should call and come in if they could. My mom was a housekeeper at Marion Manor Nursing Home in South Boston and worked there for many years. She also made a lot of friends there. She was providing the best she could for all four of us kids, and as a single mother, not once did she ever complain. Not once. Everyone that worked there loved her. They all knew Adria as the small Italian lady with the strong accent.

My mother had told me that when she was a young woman, she lived a pretty hard life. I remember her sharing with me one day that she had a job squashing grapes with her feet in Italy as a young woman. I thought to myself, that's kind of odd, given the standards of wine making today. My mother was born in 1927 in Rome, Italy, and at that time work was hard to come by. It was around the time of the Great Depression. It most certainly didn't help matters that Italy was under the fascist dictatorship of Mussolini. My mom would tell me about her father's personal and heroic sacrifice during the Holocaust.

She only had a fifth-grade education when we came to the United States. My father was an American Naval officer, which automatically gave us dual citizenship as a family. The women would line up in Naples, which was an American seaport at that time, to try and meet a man to have a better life in America. That's how they met. I was all but three years old when my brothers and I came over to America shortly after President Kennedy was assassinated in November of 1963.

It was still snowing pretty hard out, and I couldn't believe my mother was going to try and make it in to work. Little did we know that we were about to experience the worst blizzard of our lifetime. My mom, who everyone fondly remembers as Andria, was all of four feet eleven inches tall. I tried telling her that she was no match for the snow drifts as I looked out my window. Some of them were taller than her! Looking out over those fresh white mounds of powder, I could see clearly that she was at the very least going to have her hands full. She wouldn't listen to me as she started getting dressed for work. She was by all accounts and all definitions a classic stubborn Italian woman.

At the time, we lived in the D Street housing development in South Boston, or the projects, as it was called. Regardless of the storm and magnitude of it, my mother would give her all and try to make it to work. I am sure to this day it was for the extra money she would try to make as a single parent. Now I know where my drive comes from. My mom was a single parent on welfare trying to raise four kids in a town run by a gangster named Whitey Bulger. My dad had taken off and left all of us behind when we were much younger. It was in large part due to his alcoholism. They both agreed to a divorce after my father would traumatize my mom for the last time. I remember the incident as if it were yesterday, and it would be the final straw for my mother. It's like a video that keeps playing itself over and over again in my head. My dad had been home for a short period of time, and it wasn't uncommon for him to be at sea for 9 months at a time. As a matter of fact, it was typical.

I had never asked him personally, but only God knows how he got a job as a bartender at the Officers Club in South Boston. He must have known some people up the chain of command, so to speak. If there ever was a job that he should have never ever had, that was it.

We lived in the Squantum Naval housing development in Quincy at that time, and we were all still young children. We were not prepared for what we were about to witness. It was late at night as we were all sleeping when we were suddenly woken up by a crashing sound and what sounded like breaking dishes to me. We all jumped out of our beds and ran to the top of the stairs. It was then that we saw our dad leaned over our mom at the bottom of the stairs. He was taking her head by the sides of her hair and banging her forehead on the stairs. My two brothers ran back to their room as I stood paralyzed and frozen in disbelief. I couldn't believe what was happening right in front of my eyes. I was into martial arts and Bruce Lee at the time, and I remember wanting to jump off the top of the stairs and do a flying side kick on my dad as hard as I could. I was mad as hell at what I was seeing. My mom was a lot smaller than he was as he was just under six feet tall. When they realized I was still standing there at the top of the stairs watching everything that was going on, that's when my mom raised her head and said, "Johnny, go to bed." With her loving eyes she said, "It's all right, just go to bed." I paused for about ten seconds and then reluctantly I did.

As I got up the next morning, I could see through my window all of my father's clothes spewed on the front lawn and cut in half for all to see. I must admit I worried about my mom's health that morning but after looking out my window I chuckled. I said to myself, "Now, that's an Italian "woman."

I knew even as a child that the end of their marriage was near. I remember all of us kids meeting with my mom and dad not too long after and dad asking all of us children one by one whom we wanted to live with. It was no surprise to me that we all chose our mom. As I think back now over forty-five years ago, I remember my late dad saying to my older brother Jimmy, who was considered an Irish twin to me, "Jimmy, you're the oldest and in charge now. You're the man of the family, and I'm counting on you to step up in my absence." Jimmy abruptly said, "No way!" It was then that I instinctively knew that I would carry the burden of becoming the father of the family, so to speak. I wasn't going to let my mom travel alone on this new and uncertain road in a foreign land. Especially after what I had just witnessed!

As time passed on, my mom and I would become much closer and develop a special bond together. When asked where I grew up, I would often say in South Boston. Although we were born in Naples, Italy, my father would eventually dump us all in the middle of the D street projects of South Boston. Growing up in an Irish Catholic community and coming from Italy in the 1970s obviously had its challenges. We eventually came to know what was meant by the slogan "the fighting Irish." We learned that cultural mentality, especially during the Saint Patrick's Day parade. Part of our initiation of acceptance, if you will, was to start a fight during the parade. It was all part of the lower end or D street culture of Southie. We had a reputation of being a pretty tough town.

It was families like the Maher's who wrapped their loving arms around us when we first came to South Boston. We really didn't know or were friends with anyone just yet. We had lived in the same building as the Maher's, but we lived on the third floor, and they lived on the second. They were accepting of our family in every way. From our mom and all four of us children we all remember the Maher family with great fondness. Bob and Betty, or Tootsie, as we called her, were dearest to my mother and me. Betty had passed away less than a year ago, as I write. Heaven will never be the same with these two bests of friends happy and reunited once again.

My dad was Irish, from Holbrook, Massachusetts, and my mom was from Rome, Italy. Talk about opposites attracting! Maybe that's why my wife and I get along so well. I heard the door close that morning and I knew that my mom had just left and was on her way to work. I popped out of bed and went to the window to see if I could see my short little mom as she left. I knew that battling the power of Mother Nature's wind and snow would be difficult, but you just couldn't tell her. She was known as a feisty Italian woman by some and especially us kids after witnessing my father's drinking problem.

From where we lived it was less than about a quarter mile to Marion Manor Nursing Home, or a 25-to-30-minute walk on a clear day. Given the blizzard and current climate conditions, we did expect some sort of delay in hearing from mom. As I looked out my partially snow-covered window, I could see her cross the wintery roadways as she struggled to walk across D and 6th Street. I watched until I couldn't see her anymore. Now there was nothing more to do than play the waiting game for her to call. We were all really worried about mom and just wanted to know that she made it there safely. We weren't too concerned when the first forty-five minutes had passed with no call, figuring it was going to take longer than expected to get to work, especially under those wintery and harsh conditions. I had never seen so much snow piled up like this before. All the news channels were broadcasting live pictures of just how bad the blizzard had become. When an hour and a half had passed, I got a little worried and wondered why she had not called us. So, I called her work, Marion Manor, and they told me that she had not made it there yet. Now I was really worried.

Then the phone rang. Please try to remember computers and cell phones were not available back then in the 70s, and it was a much different world at that time. On the other end of the phone was Paul Cirignano, a good friend and coworker. Paul was an assistant cook in the kitchen at Marion Manor along with Mr. Greene. Paul said with a chuckle in his voice, "John, she almost made it. Your mom is safe with us, so there is no need to worry. I saw her struggling, and I figured she was trying to make it to work as she was heading up that way. I didn't think your mom would have made it as she was really laboring with the snow and wind. So, I noticed it was her and said, 'Andria,' as I was shoveling the snow off my front stairs. 'What the heck are you doing out here?' I let her know that it was not a good idea to try and make it up to work as she seemed almost totally exhausted. Being a smaller lady, I didn't think she would have the energy to continue. You know, John, that I would always take your mom in without question.

Paul had lived on 6th Street with his parents and was on the direct path my mother was walking to work. Paul and his family were gracious enough to keep my mom and take good care of her for the next three days. The entire Cirignano family were a true Godsend, for which I will always be grateful. Little did I realize that the storm would rage for days dumping just over 27.1 inches in Boston with some drifts as tall as cars. Afterward I think a lot of people including me were surprised at the length and magnitude of the storm. Don't get me wrong, being a typical seventeen-year-old at that time, I loved seeing all the snow that had fallen and just wanted to go out and play in it. Seeing all the city snowplows and private contractors would be the norm for all of us, as we just spent the last three days cooped up together watching the snow pile up.

Everything was closed, and there was no school to the delight of many. It was now time to go out and play. I remember jumping into a snow pile that was just under the height of my chin. When I did, I bounced off the pile in a funny sort of way. Little did I know, there was a small car underneath it. That's how much snow had fallen from this Nor'easter. I went back in the house around lunch time to get something to eat when the phone rang. I grabbed it thinking it was my mom, but it was a friend of mine instead. It was Donna, asking if she could get a ride home from work since her parents couldn't pick her up because of the snow and their age. After all, being almost eighteen and recently getting my license, you didn't have to ask me twice. So, I picked her up from Marion Manor just after 3:00

o'clock and started to drive her home to Dorchester. I got onto Columbia Road and headed up toward Franklin Park. From there, Donna had to give me directions to her house since I hadn't been there before. So, I drove up Columbia Road for a bit, and she said to take the next left after the bridge overpass. So, I did. We pulled up to her house on the left, and she was happy to be home safely. She thanked me for the ride home as I said, "You're welcome." I pulled away and drove back onto Columbia Road heading toward home.

As I got closer to Southie, I said to myself, "Why not go cruising down the beach?" After all, I had been there many times before, growing up as a kid, and thought it would be cool to drive and see all the snow there. I would also be able to see any damage done to the upper end or the rich section of town since it was along the coastline. I had just come off Columbia Road and onto Day Boulevard by the State Police Station and noticed there were no cars on the road at all. You certainly didn't see this every day. I had been around that rotary many times as a child, and it was always bustling with cars. So, I went by the Police station and Carson Beach, and I noticed all the snow mounds were piled up to about ten feet tall in the beach parking lots. It was clear to me that the large plows put whatever snow they could in the back of these lots. As I cruised along the two-mile stretch of coastline, I could see the majesty of the snow as I got closer to L Street. Right across on my right side was the L Street bath house, a well-known and popular destination for visitors and townies alike. I then went through the lights and drove straight ahead going by the two yacht clubs on the beach and coming up to the slight lefthanded turn at Pleasure Bay. As soon as I started to take that lefthanded turn, my car began to sputter and hesitate. Then, suddenly, it stalled. I got nervous and rolled to the right like you were parking your car in a spot except the spot was covered in snow. As soon I came to a stop, I tried turning the key to restart my car. It kept trying to turn over and over making a repetitive sound, which was becoming slower and slower. I then turned the key off and figured I would give it a little time and try again in a couple of minutes. I was also trying to save some battery life. I had no way of just calling home or anyone else for help. It was starting to get colder and darker out as night fell. I tried to start the car again, and then the battery died. With no electricity and no heat in the car, I began to shiver a bit as the temperature started to drop inside. I tried to think of any scenario that I could and kept coming up with the same one. Just wait in the car and someone would eventually come by. I wasn't dressed properly to venture out in the deep snow and cold, especially with no one around. So, I waited and waited and began shivering more and more as time passed on. I could feel my body getting colder. I folded my arms around my chest and put my hands under my armpits to try and keep warm. I don't remember any vehicles driving by and I started to become discouraged. I thought to myself that this would be a terrible way to die and to boot, I just got my license! I got to the point of shivering so bad that I really thought this would be it, and this would be the way they would find me.

It was just then when I saw a pair of headlights in my rearview mirror coming around the bend. I had positioned my mirror towards my right passenger seat side so I could see any vehicles that might be coming around the lefthanded turn at Pleasure Bay. I couldn't move enough to get out and wave down whoever it was because I was shivering so badly. It was like I was almost paralyzed and fixated on my steering wheel. At first, I thought it might be a city worker patrolling the beach area after the storm for cars like mine. But then, suddenly, the door flew open, and I heard a voice yell, "Johnny, is that you? I thought that was your car. Are you alright?"

I said that I was very cold. I forget who he had with him, but he said to him, "Help me to get Johnny out of the car." So, whoever it was that helped him, they got me into their car. I remember one of the first things I felt was the beautiful presence of warmth. First, I felt it directly on my face and eventually my whole body. By the time we got home, I was thawed out enough to make the trek up the two flights of project stairs. As I look back on that fateful night, I realize now more than ever before how my pride had almost cost me my life. I realize now just how graceful, loving, and forgiving my God is. You don't always know that God is there on your behalf, and it may not even seem like He is. But He is. It was my friend Ricky who noticed my yellow Ford Ltd, not a city worker.

UP IN SMOKE

WHEN I THINK BACK TO WHEN I WAS A YOUNG MAN, I remember a time when several of us good friends worked at the J.J. Daly Co. in South Boston. We would all meet up, and I would drive my red body, white top 1969 Volkswagen Van, pick up the boys and off to work we went. Brian had been there for several years before we came along. I remember Brian got his nickname because he had large ears just like the mice cartoon Pixie and Dixie. We would then always call Brian Pixie from that point on. His older brother Paul was nicknamed after the great M.L.B. player Boog Powell, because he was kind of built like him. Whiffle Ball was one of our favorite games to play along with half ball and off the point in the D Street projects.

The 1970s held a lot of great memories for many of us. My older brother Jimmy was nicknamed Carl Yastrzemski because he held his hands together like the famous Boston Baseball icon. The only problem was that he held them backwards when he was up at bat. I still remember to this day the boys chanting whenever Jimmy got up, "Boom, Boom, Boom, Carl Yastrzemski, Boom, Boom, Boom, Carl Yastrzemski." My younger brother Joe was nicknamed Yoyo. You could say he had his ups and downs. They even had a nickname for me, Little Sally Saucer. I thought it was because I would go to the corner store for a lot of the mothers even when they would stick their head out the project window and ask me too. I guess you could say that I had great respect for my elders at a young age, and my friends just didn't understand that about me. At least that's what I thought. As a matter of fact, it wasn't until late 2019, before the fall, that my brother Jimmy told me that my friends thought I was gay. I was stunned to say the least. Now it makes a lot of sense some forty-plus years later why I was not included in a lot of things with the boys. That was the real reason for my nickname. I was sort of quiet and introverted to a degree, given the nature of my father's alcoholism and the memory of what he did to my mom. Knowing what I know now as a former Christian Celebrate Recovery leader for over seven years, it most certainly is understandable how that specific memory can and did affect me in the way it has. It wasn't because I was gay, because I wasn't and never have been.

One of my best friends ended up being Kevin, who lived on Dorchester Street in Southie. His mother, June, was so nice and polite and a pleasure to be around. I met Kevin in work at Marion Manor Nursing Home as a kitchen worker. Now that I've had the chance to look back at my life, Kevin wasn't accepted by many people either. It kind of made me feel like the scene out of *Rudolph the Red Nosed Reindeer* when they land on the island of misfit toys. Whenever we would go to work at J.J. Daly's I still remember little Frankie calling my vehicle the peace van with the big steering wheel. He would always be good for a laugh.

Being the main disc jockey at Triple O's in Southie came with its natural, unforeseen problems as I hung around the place too much. Being close to the D Street projects where I lived surely didn't help matters at all. I remember that before me getting the job at Triple O's, South Boston was often on television's national scene, because we were the epicenter of forced busing. I was a graduate of South Boston High School class of 1979 and lived through what is known as the experimental integration age. I am not and never was a racist during that most difficult time. My God is color-blind, and so am I. It truly wasn't a good learning environment for me or any of the students at South Boston High School. Having the tactical police force lining the hallways in full riot gear between class exchanges at the ringing of the bells, was a vivid visual reminder of just how far down the racial divide we had fallen.

My best friend in the world was a black man, and his name is Jake Coakley, who has since gone home to be with the Lord. Jake was also working in the cotton fields down south trying to support his family and gave up any hope he had of educating himself. Jake, unbeknownst to me, could not read until he graduated from the W.A.I.T.T. house in Roxbury, Massachusetts. I truly do miss him a lot. I first met Jake working on the state-of-the-art Deer Island Sewage Plant as a proud member of Carpenters Local 33 at the time. We would also be cleaning up Boston Harbor as a result. We were partners, and frequently took the Deer Island Ferry across Boston Harbor to work from Quincy. Jake would try and explain the Trinity to me as I was struggling to try and understand the concept of three people in one. Jake wasn't always the easiest man to understand, but by the time he was done explaining the Trinity to me, I clearly understood. Jake was a good man, a good friend, and someone I looked up to.

At that time and as a DJ, I belonged to the Boston Record Pool located in Kenmore Square. I got a lot of new releases even before some of them hit the store shelves. I remember going into Tower Records off Massachusetts Ave. just down the street from Berkley College of music. As a DJ, I was always trying to stay on top of all the new and popular dance music that was coming out. Disco dance music was the craze at that time and was still extremely popular. Madonna was a rising and budding star just topping the charts back then. Between the record pool and Tower Records, you could always get a copy of a twelve-inch vinyl version or an extended dance mix version of a popular song. E.U. Wurlitzer was also another place I would frequently visit to stay on top of what was new in electronics. Since they were located right around the corner from Tower Records and may have been connected to the same building, it made a lot of sense to plan to visit them both together. One day, I went down to Triple O's to drop off some of the newest hits I had just bought from Tower Records. When you come into Triple O's lounge, as you first walk in the door and to your immediate right is an entrance with a sliding glass–style door. Behind that door is a stairwell to the second-floor function room, where I would be the entertainment at private parties at times. It was also the back of the bar wall. As you walked in you had the bar on your righthand side stretching down about seventy feet or so down to the dance floor. On the left-hand side, you would have all your seating with tables scattered all the way down to where the bar ended. Then, you would have a small section of L-shaped style seating near the DJ booth, where I played. You always had to hop up onto the seating and into the DJ booth. At the very end of the small booth, where the mixer and the turntables were located, there was a set of stairs that led down to the bathrooms. That basically was the layout of the Triple O's lounge back then.

I remember it was a warm summer day when I went in the O's one late afternoon to drop off some records to add to my collection. Workers and patrons alike called the main bartender and cook during the day "Fitzy". You could say he was a perma-nent fixture there. He was always in there for many years and known as a steady worker. I would say that there were under ten people in the bar, which wasn't unusual for that time of day. I went in to drop off some records, and as I was talking to Fitzy at the bar, I overheard a conversation of the two guys sitting right next to me. One of them said he was off to work at the Channel nightclub in Boston, and he had better start walking if he wanted to get there on time. I said to him, "Excuse me. I wasn't eavesdropping on your conversation, but I did hear you say you were going to walk down to the Channel nightclub. Is that right?" He replied, "Yeah, I am." I then said to him, "if you would like a ride to the Channel, I don't mind dropping you off. I am leaving anyway. I know the club well, as me and my friends go there occasionally."

He said, "sure, if you don't mind." I said, "I don't mind at all. I have the red Volkswagen van parked right out front. No rush. Take your time. I'll be outside." So, I left the O's hopped into my van and started her up. He then came out a couple minutes later and hopped into the passenger side. He said, "you sure you don't mind?" "No, not at all," I said. So, I banked a U-turn in front of Triple O's heading down West Broadway to the lights at A Street. I said to him as we were taking the left onto A Street with Ambrein's Restaurant on our right, "Did you know that Ambrein's is the oldest restaurant in South Boston?" He said no that he didn't know. I said, "It sure is, and it's been around since 1890. Being from Southie I'm full of useless information like that." He chuckled. He said that he would be a little early since he was getting a ride, but that he didn't mind at all. "It sure beats walking about a mile to work," he said. We got about halfway there, and I said to him, "I remember when the great Roy Orbison played at the Channel this past winter in December. It was the talk of the town. I remember my older brother Jimmy telling me that he and his friends went down to the Channel one night clubbing and got into a fight with several kids from Charlestown in the parking lot. He told me that someone hit him in the back with a tire jack, and he was saved by his friends Joe, Buffy, and Eddie, who also fought to save my brother. They helped get Jimmy back to his car, and they all went home. Jimmy was sore and licking his wounds for several days after. So, we are awfully familiar with the Channel Nightclub I said as we pulled up to its front door. He thanked me again and that would be the last time I would ever see him.

I pulled away from the Channel nightclub and was heading back down A Street. When I drove down the mile or so to the lights at the intersection of A Street and West Broadway, the lights turned yellow and then red. I slowed down and came to a complete stop at the red light. Then, suddenly, I heard a loud boom in the back of the van and the wind inside thrust my upper body into the large steering wheel as I closed my eyes in reaction. I opened my eyes blinking them rapidly and wondered what the hell just happened. Did I get hit from behind? Then, suddenly, thick gray smoke began slowly oozing up and out my vents that are normally used for defrosting located on the topside of my dashboard. I knew this wasn't good. I instinctively turned the key off and jumped out my driver's door so fast, I didn't even close the door. The entire van went up in flames in about three minutes. There were flames coming out of every direction as the van was now fully engulfed. I heard the fire engines coming down the street from the D Street firehouse just minutes away. They came quickly, but by the time they arrived the van was a burning inferno and a total loss. I was totally stunned watching my van burn to the ground. I was standing on the Ambrein's side of the sidewalk watching the firefighters as they rolled out their hose and began spraying my van down with water. Then, one of the firefighters holding the hose yelled over to me, "Hey kid, is this your vehicle?" I stared at him with a blank look on my face and then slowly nodded yes. He then said, "Do you have insurance on it?" I hesitated for a couple of seconds and shook my head side to side a few times without saying a word. He then said, "Get out of here, kid!" So, I ran home.

FOR MY EYES ONLY

SOMETIMES ON OUR JOURNEY OF EVERYDAY LIVING comes a real-life incident that can shape and mold who we are to become. For me, this is one of those events. It was a beautiful sunny and warm summer morning, and we were going to picturesque Campton New Hampshire's Waterville Estates and lake area to spend some time with my in-laws. We had a little red 1994 Toyota Corolla sedan at that time, and Britney was our only child. In a sense it was much easier to move around back then. So, Claire packed up the car with everything we needed as she brought food, snacks, and drinks. She was the type of woman who was always prepared. I don't know if it is a gender thing, like I've been told, but as far as Claire and me, she has always been the one who has paid closer attention to those kinds of details. Once we had everything packed up and ready to go, we were off to the beautiful state of New Hampshire. We got directions from Barbara and we were off and on our way.

I remember driving the about two-hour drive and thinking to myself, this is taking an awful long time to get there. I don't know if it was my impatience or the fact that I hadn't been there before. Claire's sister, Barbara, had rented a three-story townhouse that seemed like it was in the middle of the woods at Waterville Estates. It was a planned vacation for her mom Barbara Sr., her sister Karen, and young daughter Elizabeth, along with us three. The homes looked like three side-by-side townhomes together with a dumpster outside. The renters said to Barbara, "Just be careful of the bears at night," and being New Hampshire, we weren't a bit surprised. When we finally got there, we parked near the lake area. We then grabbed all our beach stuff and Britney and headed to Campton pound. Claire was carrying Britney, so I was double fisted with the rest of the stuff. As we got to the sandy part of the lake where Barbara Sr., Elizabeth, and Barbara were all spread out on a blanket, we set up right next to them. Then, I thought about something that had been eating away at me for some time now. The fact that as a man I had been surrounded by women and their opinions for most of my life. As a man, I felt all alone with no male to talk to or bounce ideas off. My wife was a female, her mom was a female, Barbara was a female, Claire's sister Karen was a female, Karen's daughter was a female, and we had our daughter Britney at that time. There were just no males in my life that I could express myself to or bounce ideas off. My younger brother was living in the state of Virginia, and my older brother was A.W.O.L. from my family. I haven't seen or talked to Jimmy in years. So, I said to myself, "I'll show them."

As soon as we got there I pointed and told them I was going to swim to that island out there. Before anyone could say anything, or even comment, I dropped all the beach stuff right where I was standing and started running toward the lake and into the water. The splashing of my feet was driving the water in an upward direction, and when the water got to above my knees and became harder and harder to run, I dove in headfirst. I remember thrusting my arms forward like a professional swimmer and breathing on my right side every four strokes. Do not get me wrong, I am not a professional swimmer by any means, but I could swim. I remember taking swimming lessons for years at the South Boston Boys Club. I figured the island didn't look too far away and that I could swim out to it with no problem. I kept swimming and swimming and got about halfway there and started feeling a little tired. So, I began treading water and figured I would get my bearings and re-evaluate my goal. As I was treading water and seeing how much further I had to swim, I could see out of the corner of my right eye someone rowing a boat and coming toward me. One thing I must say is I have what I consider to be a gift and that is great peripheral vision. It was no secret when I was a kid and whenever we had street hockey games in South Boston, they would always ask if I was going to play or not. I had an uncanny ability to seem like I was stick handling going toward the net and was able to dish a pass off on my left or right side to an oncoming player. Because of my peripheral vision I was able to fake out and draw more than enough players toward me while dishing off a pass to an oncoming player. It usually resulted in a high percentage goal shot. You could say I had a high number of assists.

The boat got to about six feet from me when I turned slightly to my right while treading water. I could see clearly that it was a young girl about ten or twelve years old with what looked like two new wooden oars. The boat was about eight to ten feet long and made of very shiny aluminum. I remember because the sun was glistening off it and it looked brand new. The girl had blond hair down to her shoulders and blue eyes. She had on a white dress with what looked like one to one and a half inchwide straps on her shoulders. She said to me, "Do you know how deep it is out here?" I replied, "No, but it must be pretty deep." She said, "Yeah, it is." "Well, Id' better turn around and go back then." She said, "Yeah, I would." So, I started to turn around when suddenly, my arms felt like they weighed 1000 pounds each. No mattered how hard I tried to lift my arms up off my sides, I couldn't. They went all the way down my sides like I was standing straight up at attention. I began to sink slowly downward frantically kicking my feet to try and stay afloat. My call for help didn't come out very loud but loud enough for Barbara and Claire to hear. Barbara asked Claire if she thought I was kidding as she gave Britney over to her mother. Claire said no. Oh my God, I think he's drowning! They both ran in to the lake with Barbara slightly ahead of Claire. I kept my eyes open as I began to sink under water. I remember feeling the water rise above my lips, nose, and then I could see underwater. I then closed my eyes and thought I am surely going to die because there was absolutely nothing I could do physically to stay afloat. As soon as I closed my eyes, I heard a swooshing of water just above my head and then felt an arm wrap around my neck under the water.

The next thing I knew I was on my back above water and opened my eyes facing the sky. I was being pulled toward the shore by someone who saw me treading water and struggling to stay afloat. Two men had jumped in quickly and swam by Barbara and Claire. They had been swimming that lake numerous times over a five year period and said it was deep where I was. We would learn all of this after I was pulled to safety, and I truly hope to meet them one day. That is my sincere hope. I would like to thank both men for being part of God's bigger plan for me and saving my life. After they had pulled me to shore, I sat there with my knees to my chest as a waiting ambulance was about forty feet to my left. They asked me if I wanted to be checked out in the ambulance, and I said, "No, I'm fine, I really am. I am more embarrassed than anything else. But I'm fine really. Thank you, thank you guys."

I spent about a minute or two just thinking and mulling over what just had happened. I turned to my left and said to Claire, "I am really sorry for what I did, and I'm so sorry for putting you and Britney through this. It was undoubtedly my pride as a man that got the best of me. I tried to show off to all of you girls thinking I would make it to the island out there. I am so, so sorry. If it wasn't for that little girl in the aluminum boat asking me if I knew how deep it was out there and with a puzzled look on her face—"

Claire interrupted me and said, "John, what girl?" I didn't see any girl or boat out there." I told her again in somewhat of a surprised voice, "I'm telling you; I spoke to a little girl. She was about ten to twelve years old with blond hair and blue eyes wearing a pure white dress with shoulder straps. She had shoulder-length hair and was rowing an aluminum boat." Again, Claire said she did not see any boat or any person out there. I turned to Barbara, her sister, and asked her the same thing. She said, "John, I honestly don't remember seeing a little girl or any rowboat out there either." I was stunned. They both did not see the girl I spoke to as I was treading water. As true as the sun is in the sky, so was my encounter with that blond-hair little girl in the rowboat in the white dress. I am reminded of the scripture that says,

Then Jesus told him, "Because you have seen me, you have believed; blessed are those who have not seen and yet have believed" (John 20:29 NIV).

SECOND CHANCES

SOME OF US LOOK AT LIFE CIRCUMSTANTIALLY OR the here and now, and that's all we see. That's fine. Sometimes, we look at things through the big-picture lens of life and can envision things to come. We can even understand why some things have happened to us. That's fine too. I have learned being married twenty-eight years this past June and going out with my wife five years beforehand. I am a big-picture guy. I am not saying that one way is better than the other, because that would be wrong of me. I also believe it is without question for me anyway, a gift from God. For some time now, I've had my own DJ business and have done pretty well. I had attended and graduated from Northeast Broadcasting School fresh out of South Boston High with hopes of becoming a radio personality. I remember one of my instructors telling all of us students about New England regionalisms and the difference between Bostonians and the rest of the radio world. One thing for sure is that they did not mix well together at all. In major market radio, if you wanted a job on the air you had better get rid of what is known as your Boston accent. In other words, pronounce the words as they are spelled. We as New Englanders have a tendency not to enunciate the very end of words like words ending in -er or -ing. If you spell them out correctly like mother, father, sister, brother, computer, or teacher, you will notice they all have an er on the end. We tend to pronounce them here in New England like they were spelled, mothah, fathah, sistah, brothah, computah, and teachah. What happened to the er? Did it just magically fall off? We also tend to do the same thing for words ending in ing. Words like playing, staying, laying, falling, and running. We pronounce them like playin', stayin', layin', fallin', and runnin'. Did the "g" fall off? That in large part is what is known throughout the industry as New England regionalisms.

I graduated Northeast Broadcasting School and then applied and landed an apprenticeship position at KISS 108 FM. As producer of the extremely popular Sonny Joe White show, it was quite a big deal for me coming out of a small broadcasting school in Boston on Marlborough Street. Landing an internship on the number-one radio station in Boston gave me instant popularity. I thought I was on my way to my dream job and even had a stage name or radio name all picked out: John Roberts. Here I was the producer of the 6 p.m. to 9 p.m., Monday through Friday, Sonny Joe White show and working at the number-one contemporary radio station in Boston. Those are surprisingly good credentials, I thought.

Working there came with its perks as well. I would go to countless KISS concerts and meet some of the hottest bands and groups of the time. On top of all that I owned my own DJ business and played at the infamous Triple O's lounge Thursday through Sunday nights. Whenever I couldn't play at the O's I would always do the responsible thing and get coverage for myself. I played at many weddings, christenings, anniversaries, birthday parties, benefits, and more during my DJ career.

One night I was scheduled to play at a birthday party in Whitman. I remember getting hired through a longtime friend of mine, Debbie Hogue. I had also played at Debbie and Tim's wedding celebration. My best friend Ricky was going to Rhode for me that night, so we loaded up the van with all my gear, which was heavy and was not easy. I had a large pair of Peavey speakers, a coffin as we called it back then, with two Technique 1200 turntables and a mixer inside. Believe it or not we played vinyl records back then. I played everything from Big Bands, 50s music, Frank Sinatra, Motown, and pop music. Madonna was just coming onto the pop scene as a rising star. It may be hard to understand by today's social media standards, but back then we didn't have MP3s, memory sticks, or CDs. Downloading anything wasn't even possible, and we used fish tubs containers to store records. Believe me when I say to you that they were heavy. It's not like today's DJs, who can just use a laptop and download all of the music they want. Just get an amplifier for volume, plug in a smaller pair of speakers, and you are well on your way. We will not even mention the amount of money they are getting today.

It was just before the sun was setting, and we were about to get underway to the birthday party in Whitman. There was a light blanket of snow on the ground, after all, it was wintertime. I turned the radio on to my favorite station, KISS 108 FM, and we were off to Debbie's friend's birthday party in Whitman. Ricky lit up a smoke as we headed for the South East expressway toward the split in Braintree at Route 3. I had planned to get off in Weymouth and up Route 18 to Whitman. There wasn't anything unusual other than the fact it was snowing a bit on the expressway. As we passed Dorchester into Quincy, the traffic at that time was just a bit slower than usual because of the falling snow. When we went by East Milton square and drove further up toward the split as it bears left onto Route 3 to Cape Cod, the cars in front us began slowing down. We slowed down and eventually came to a stop in the fast lane just when you take the left-hand turn onto Route 3. The Southeast Expressway had turned into what looked like a big parking lot. Cars sat still for as far as the eye could see. I remember looking out to my driver's side window and seeing the intersecting expressway bustling with cars directly underneath us.

We were sitting there for about a minute when suddenly, we were hit from behind and jolted slightly forward. I said a few choice words to myself and then got out on the driver's side. Ricky got out on the passenger side safely as all traffic had come to a complete stop. As I approached the car that hit us, I realized it was what looked like a Ford Pinto. I then saw a smaller guy get out on the driver's side, he had black hair and was about five and a half feet tall. He was about twenty to twenty-three years old and was a little shorter than me. Then

I saw this huge guy get out on the passenger side. I said to myself, "Oh boy, I hope we don't have any problems with this guy, or we're in some serious trouble." We first went to see if there was any damage to my vehicle as we both looked at the back of my van and then the front of his car. The impact propelled my van forward just missing the car in front of me. Since they were both older vehicles and there was no serious damage, there was no need to exchange papers for such a small fender bender I said. It wouldn't be worth the insurance because both vehicles were older. "I'm really sorry I slid into you. It really was my fault" he said. I said to him, "Do not worry about it, there's no harm done."

Traffic was just starting to move when the bigger guy was bent over, and it looked like he was trying to find scratches or further damage on his car. Ricky yelled, "Johnny, look out!" I immediately looked to my right and saw a white customized van sliding out of control at the bend heading right toward me and his car. It was like a slow-motion video. To this day, I remember vividly seeing the two back full-view driver's side windows with two beautiful white Akita dogs sitting straight up in them. I remember seeing one in each seat as it was sliding and heading toward me. Out of instinct, I turned further to my right and jumped onto the top of the concrete Jersey barrier beside me. I immediately started leaning toward the expressway below, which was about a thirty-to-forty-foot drop. As I was leaning over and heading downward toward the expressway below, which had a lot of cars traveling on it, I grabbed the back of the signage so hard with both hands and pulled myself in as tight as I could. I closed my eyes bracing for some type of impact. That's when I heard the white van crash into the back of the Ford Pinto propelling it into my van. With my eyes still tightly closed, I then felt the driver's side mirror of the out-of-control van just brush the back of my shirt as I stood holding tightly the back of the expressway bellows signage. It was then I heard a person crying out, "Mommy, mommy, mommy, please help me, help me, mommy," screaming and groaning in pain. After the immediate danger had passed, I kept hearing the cries for help, I opened my eyes and hopped down from the Jersey barrier and onto the expressway to see if I could help. At that time, the expressway was blanketed by less than two inches of snow. It was the big guy that got out of the Ford Pinto's passenger side and was looking for further damage on his vehicle that got hurt. Unfortunately, he was still between the two vehicles at the time and got caught between my van and his car. Thank God Ricky and the driver of the Ford Pinto did not get hurt. The big guy's legs were crushed from the crash.

The State Police came quickly along with an ambulance. I gave an account to the State Police officer of what had happened as the ambulance paramedics attended to the big guy, who was injured and in pain. I had also explained to him I had to get to a birthday party in Whitman as I was the disc jockey entertainment, and that people were waiting for me. The State Trooper said, "We have all the information we need. Just make sure to contact your insurance company and let them know what happened." I said, "Thank you, officer. If you don't mind," I asked him, "Would you please tell the driver of the Ford Pinto I can't stay because I'm expected to play at a friend's birthday party in Whitman?" The officer said that he would, and I was quickly on my way as there was nothing more that I could do.

Obviously, being traumatized by the accident itself was a lot for me to handle. Almost falling forty feet below onto another expressway was very upsetting and made me even more anxious, never mind being late for a birthday party. I remember my friend Debbie was extremely nervous because I had not arrived on time, and who could blame her. When we got there, Debbie said that Ricky and I looked pretty shaken up and nervous. I then explained what had happened on our way there, and they said, "Oh my God!" They then understood the circumstances and reason for our late arrival. As I look back now, I realize how much more graceful, merciful, loving, and kind my God is. He truly is a God of second chances.

MISTAKEN IDENTY

SOMETIMES IN LIFE A MEMORY OR EVENT MAY REAR its ugly head when triggered by someone or something. Having come from a military family with my dad serving in Vietnam, among other places, it seems somehow fitting to recall that horrible and terrifying memory. Like many of our veterans who are suffering from PTSD, I too struggle with the memory of that early Saturday South Boston morning. It was a typical Friday night as I was playing at Triple O's lounge on West Broadway in South Boston. I must admit I did gain some notoriety at the now infamous Triple O's lounge. You might say that there's a lot of history there. Most of the regulars were friends of mine, and some were just people I knew. It didn't hurt my notoriety to any degree that I worked at the number-one pop radio station in Boston, KISS 108 FM. Given that I was Sonny Joe White's producer, who was an extremely popular disc jockey at the time, would just add to my popularity. I landed that job as a graduate of Northeast Broadcasting School on Marlboro Street in Boston.

I had just wrapped up another Friday night of patrons drinking, dancing, and having fun at Triple O's. It was about

2:30 in the morning as I was leaving the bar, and my best friend Ricky was waiting for me outside. He was driving a car with one other person in the back seat. I came out and hopped in the front seat, and we began to pull away from the O's heading down West Broadway to the lights. I remember saying to Ricky, "Where we headed to?" He said down the beach to meet Ronso and others. We used to go there a lot after work to get high, drink, or just hang out to the early morning hours. So, I said cool as we took a left at the lights and made our way up Dorchester Ave. We weren't on the Ave for more than twenty seconds when I saw a white car behind us in my passenger side mirror. Ricky moved over to the right lane just being courteous to let him go by. The car then switched lanes and ended up behind us once again. I said, "Ricky I think we're being followed for some reason. Switch over to the left lane," and so he did. We were coming up to a four-way traffic light, which remained green, so we took a left-hand turn onto Dorchester Street, and the car was still tailing us. It seemed like this car was behind us forever as we switched over to the right lane, and then the white car did the same. Now I started to get a little more nervous and anxious as I wondered why the heck we were being followed. We had made it all the way up to the intersection of West and East Broadway, and took a right-hand turn switching lanes again on East Broadway. We went by Walsh Insurance and then Stapleton Florists, which were well-known store fronts along that route. East Broadway is about a mile long from its beginning to end. We were traveling in the left lane as we were coming up to the traffic lights at East Broadway and L Street. The lights turned yellow as we were approaching and then red.

Ricky slowed down and came to a complete stop. The white car was still right behind us. Then, suddenly, and out of the blue the car darted to the right lane and pulled up right beside my window. The white male I'd say was in his early forties with black curly hair. He was signaling to me to roll down my window. So, I did. As soon as I did, I could hear him loudly, and I knew that he was upset about something. We were face to face with only about two feet separating both of us. He started to yell at me saying, "You stole my radio, yeah it was you." I was very, surprised as I was never accused of stealing anyone's radio. I replied, "Hey, buddy, I didn't steal your radio. I just got out of work at Triple O's. I am the disc jockey there, and my name is John Broderick. There is no way buddy, no way I stole your radio. It had to be somebody else." He said loudly, "No, I know it was you" and pulled out a handgun from his waist area pointed it against my right temple. He screamed at the top of his lungs and yelled, "Ahhhhhhh." I closed my eyes thinking I was going to die right then and there with a bullet in my head. I heard the blast and kept my eyes closed for about three to five seconds. Then, I opened my eyes, blinking them quickly and nervously. As soon as everything came into focus, I remember seeing the trunk of the white car speeding away. It was then, with my mind racing that I looked around and saw that there was no blood and nobody else in the car was hurt. I realized he had shot straight up in the air with the gun close to my ear.

The person in the back was smart enough to take down the white car's license plate. I've got to say that when a gun goes off that close to your ear, it's a heart-pounding event. I never in a million years would have guessed that I was going to die that way. After that fateful morning, my ear was ringing for about a week. The next day or Sunday afternoon I went to my boss and told him what had happened. He was incredibly surprised that it happened and especially to me. I explained to him that one of the other guys in the back took down the license plate number of the car. So, I gave him the note with the license plate number on it. He said, "John, come down Monday afternoon and we'll see who the car belongs to." I said, "OK, I'll make sure that I'm there." So, I came outside of Triple O's just as he told me on that Monday. I saw the white car pull up shortly after, and the man with the curly black hair I had seen Saturday morning got out of the car. He went into Triple O's to talk to my boss to be held into account for what he had done. I had a reputation of being a good guy and a valued employee to my boss and coworkers alike at Triple O's. My boss came out and said, "John, is that him? Is that the guy and is that the car?" I nodded yes. He said, "You can leave now." I felt much relieved. So, I left Triple O's that Monday afternoon, and I don't know whatever came of that meeting. I made sure not to ask.

THE FALL CONTINUED

JUST BEFORE YOU GET INTO THE B.M.C. AREA, YOU are hit with the harsh visual reality of today's major cities John says. In Boston, what is disparagingly known as "Methadone Mile" is a stretch of land that has several homeless shelters and methadone clinics along it. It is hard for me to see all the homeless and addicted congregating on such a small parcel of land. It's an extreme vast majority of heroin addicts, male and female of all colors and nationalities, hanging out together. Ever since the demolishing of the Quincy Long Island Shelter Bridge in March 2015, they have congregated along a strip known as Methadone Mile, just a block and a half away from Boston Medical Center Hospital. My younger sister Helen had struggled with heroin addiction before succumbing to it. She also stayed at Rosie's Place, a well-known woman's homeless shelter in Boston. My beautiful niece Kimberly, Helen's daughter, died only months ago of this hideous disease. Her only surviving brother, Eddie, is getting out of prison for armed bank robbery after years of confinement due to this horrible addiction. Boston Medical Center is a world-renowned Hospital John said, and is known to many having a great reputation and justifiably so. It boasts a team of class A doctors, nurses, aides, and staff.

As they rushed John through the emergency doors, I thought he was pulling his mask off, and I believe that he was trying to say, "I love you" and that he was going to be OK Claire said. At least that is what I thought I heard him say. John was always telling me that he loved me, and everything was going to be OK. He was always the strong one both physically and mentally. I remember seeing a neck brace on him as they rushed John by. I ran alongside him, crying and praying for him saying, "I'm here, I love you, and it's going to be OK." Then the double doors shut, and I was left in the hallway alone and very scared. I felt numb and had a hollow pit in my stomach. I didn't know how severe his injuries were, but I knew they were pretty bad. Then, I placed a call to my sister Barbara, my sister Karen, and my mom telling them of what had happened. I asked my sister Barbara to pick up Brianna from work at Stop and Shop on Newport Ave in Quincy and meet us at the hospital. Robert drove himself and his Uncle Jimmy to the hospital while Britney drove herself to B.M.C. in her car.

Because of the visiting policy at the time, the nurses were only allowing two people to go back at a time. We thought it would be best for Robert and Jimmy to go in and see John. They really needed to know how he was doing since they were both there when the fall took place. When everyone else arrived, they put us all in a room by ourselves, where we would wait to hear any updates or news from the doctors. Everyone was nervously waiting, praying, and praying. I went out to the front area, because we had not heard anything for a few hours now. The last thing I was told is that they did not know if John was going to make it or not. They told the family that there was no change in his condition either. So, we were basically stuck in a verbal holding pattern of uncertainly, anxiety, and fear. I asked the people at the reception desk if they prayed, and Tina, an African American woman with a wonderful personality, who was the front receptionist, said, "I do." I said to her, "Please pray for my husband, John, because we do not know if he is going to make it or not." Tina was so nice, and she came back and prayed with us. Tina said to us, "John's really going to need all of you right now, so you all need to put on your big girl's pants."

After much time had passed, John was transported out of the ER and into the Intensive Care Unit (ICU) where Agnes, one of the most experienced nurses, would take care of him while he was in such a critical state. That night the kids and I stayed by John's side until Agnes said, "Only one person can sleep in the room." The kids wanted me to sleep in the room while they slept in the waiting room. Agnes asked me to sleep in the chair across from John, because the doctors needed the room around the bed to assess John, which they were doing every hour. Agnes told me, "Don't worry, we will take good care of him." When the kids went to the waiting room, I turned on the Christian music and started to read from the *Jesus Calling* book by Sarah Young. I remember telling John, "We are fighting for you here, but you have to fight to live." I told Britney, Brianna, and Robert that I believed "God gave John a recovery ministry, Anew Ministries Christ Centered Recovery" that he faithfully started. I don't believe at all that God would take it away from him. I believe God wanted John to fulfill it.

John was still unconscious and unresponsive as the night went on. His life was still hanging by a thread. As the night progressed, we called in the chaplains for prayer, along with Father Ignatius because of the extreme uncertainty of his health. It was at that time that Father Ignatius Nze felt he should read John his last rights. "My Father's house has many rooms; if that were not so, would I have told you that I am going there to prepare a place for you? And if I go and prepare a place for you, I will come back and take you to be with me that you also may be where I am; You know the way to the place where I am going" John 14 2–4 N.I.V. The diagnosis was still unclear and throughout the night testing would be required. John was still in a critical state, unconscious, between life and death, so I slept in the room, and the kids stayed in the waiting room with my sister and John's brother. John's brother Jimmy called his other brother Joe, who lives in Virginia, to tell him what had happened, and Joe booked a flight to come to Boston. No one knew what John's condition would be like in the next few hours. As the night went on, John would receive multiple tests including a CAT scan and frequent neurological checks to assess cognitive function. Later, the CAT scan revealed that he had four fractured upper ribs, two to five because of the fall. The tests also showed that he had bleeding on the brain. The area of the brain that was the most impacted was the deep part of the brain that is responsible for mobility and other cognitive functions. A hole was drilled toward the back right side of John's skull where an Intracranial Pressure Monitoring device was inserted to monitor pressure on his brain. We had never seen that before and it was scary to see John's head wrapped in gauze, on a breathing tube and unable to move. John was then diagnosed with a severe traumatic brain injury (TBI), paralyzing the right side of his body.

The fact that John could not move the entire right side of his body was genuinely concerning to his doctors. They said there was some bleeding on the brain, but it was not a large amount, which was kind of a good sign. Britney, Brianna, Robert, and I were so worried and upset that John was not going to make it, that we cried. What kind of life would the kids and I have without him? I kept texting Bob O'Donnell, a male nurse, over at Beth Israel Hospital in Milton. He asked me if John's brain had shifted. If it didn't, Bob said, that would be a good thing. Bob was a former captain and shift commander in the Stoughton Fire Department, and I really valued his opinion as a male nurse.

On January 6, the second day after John's terrible fall, I remember crying out to God reminding myself, God can do all things when we can't. I must trust Him in the dark. God knows we all have a lot of unanswered questions. I am here praying for a complete healing and honestly believing that God will do that for us. On this day, John opened his eyes. This was the first glimmer of hope and the very first sign we saw. It gave us all the hope that God truly was answering our prayers. God would continue to show us little victories ever since then, starting with his left foot moving while his hand was in mine. These victories would be sporadic and when the doctors were doing their routine neurological checks, they would not see the same things that we did. John would be in the intensive care unit for at least another couple of weeks, while Katherine, Bethany, Peter, Denise, and Bill would take over caring for John. They would be his new nurses and staff at this critical juncture in John's life. We called the chaplains office for continued prayer and met Chaplain Marina, Chaplain Sam, Havilah, who was a Godsend to Brianna along with Chris. Havilah was a student at Boston University and was studying to be a chaplain. She appeared to Brianna when she needed it the most and since then would be referred to as her guardian angel. We kept telling John, "You need to fight for your life, and we're all fighting for you here on the outside, but you need to fight and stay alive Claire said. When nobody has the answers, God does."

Uncle Joe flew in from Virginia on Tuesday. He asked if he could stay the night with John because he didn't know if John was going to make it. I thought it was a good idea, and I was glad Joe wanted to stay with John. We all slept in the waiting room for the first couple of nights. Every hour, consistently, the doctors kept going in trying to wake him up saying, "John, can you hear me? Hey, John, can you hear me?" There was no response at all as they were assessing him. The doctors needed to know just how alert he was, if at all, and what the neurological state of his mind was. However, he was still unconscious. One of the doctors gave John a mobility test ranging on a scale from zero to five, of which he got a zero (no mobility). They really did not know if he would ever walk, talk, or if he was permanently paralyzed. They had no answers for us. However, we knew that God did. God revealed so many things to us giving us hope, as the doctors on the other hand were painting a very grim picture of John's condition. John opened his eyes a bit more and had a little bit more mobility on the left side, however, the right side did not. We were praying for John's right side to come back and show us signs of mobility, but it did not. I was praying he would stay strong and at peace with God. I was also praying that he would not give up because, I did not want to live without him. I prayed for continued strength and that God would have His way. John opened his eyes more and was squeezing my hand with his left hand. The kids and I were seeing little miracles all throughout the day. The miracle I thought John would be the most excited about is when our daughter Brianna quoted scripture out of the blue! She quoted John 4:48, which says, "Unless you people see signs and wonders," Jesus told him, "you will never believe."

During the neurological assessment, the day after and while John was still in an unconscious state, the doctors pinched his right shoulder where he originally had no movement, and suddenly, it moved! Another miracle! The doctors said that they did not know about John's limitations and probably would not until the intubation tube came out. The doctor told us, "To prepare for the worst so when the good comes, if it comes, you will be extremely happy."

Thursday, the neck brace came off after doctors determined it was safe and that there were no spinal injuries. Praise God! I am reminded of what came from the lips of my Lord Jesus in John 16:33, "In this world you will have trouble." John had a setback and developed pneumonia. I saw tears in his eyes while I was trying to encourage him to stay strong and not give up. "You must stay strong, John," I said, "Because I love you. Britney, Brianna, and Robert love you too!" Then, I remembered the second half of John 16:33, "But take heart! I have overcome the world."

You were resting comfortably, and your white blood cell count was going down, which was a positive thing. The doctors told us that you would not be able to move on your own, but your reflexes were working. They also said that you had lost thirty pounds since the fall to 202 pounds.

It wasn't until Saturday that we met Catherine, who was an African American woman in the waiting room. Her mother unfortunately had suffered a stroke. I am so thankful that we all crossed paths and for Catherine and her brother Chris comforting Brianna during a time everyone was crying and sad. Every day we would meet in the waiting room and we would ask each other how everyone was doing. She asked about John, and they prayed for him, and we asked about her mom, and we prayed for her. Throughout this time, we were also in constant contact with the chaplains. Chaplain Sam had brought John a prayer blanket that was knitted by a 101-year-old nun named Arlene, who was out of St. Joseph's in Framingham. She knitted every single stitch with a prayer. John immediately took to the blanket and would constantly have it in his hands, feeling the texture of the stiches. Knowing how comforting it was to him, we had asked if Catherine's mom could receive one as well. Chaplain Sam said he would deliver one to her shortly after.

We were also told that the intubation tube that John had in was only supposed to stay in for fourteen days. After that, the doctors told us that he would need a tracheotomy. They told us we had one more day, and on that day, if the tube had not come out, then they would have to do the trach. I remembered John saying he did not ever want a trach because he had a friend who had it done, and his voice was never the same. So, I said do whatever you can do and if you must think outside the box, then do it. But no trach unless it's absolutely necessary. So, I texted our good friend and male nurse Bob O'Donnell at Beth Israel Milton Hospital, and he said that the trach was OK and that it could be reversed.

Two surgeons came in on Sunday, and Britney and I said to them, "What are you doing?" "We are here to check his anatomy to do a trach," they said. "Oh no, you're not! The doctor gave us until tomorrow, and we're praying that John would not need it." After the doctors had checked his airway, they said that they could not go ahead with the trach because his airway was just too difficult. Another prayer answered! The doctors were able to remove the intubation tube but had to insert a feeding tube. A couple of days had passed, and John kept pulling out the feeding tube that the doctors put in. They told us that John wasn't getting enough calories and that they may have to give him a permanent feeding bag. We kept on praying, praying, and praying, and after a few days they said they would like to take it out and put him on pureed foods. Another prayer answered.

Catherine expressed concern when she found out her mother may need a trach. Our situations were remarkably similar, and we would often share with each other the experiences our loved ones were facing. We said, "Catherine, we will pray that your mother doesn't need a trach." I remember sitting in the green chair, praying that John would not need one, and another prayer was answered. John didn't! We called the green chair "the prayer chair," and we sent it over to Catherine's mother's room, praying her mom did not need a trach either.

It has been nine days since the fall, and we were having great difficulty just trying to understand John and what his needs were. Britney suggested that they give him a laminated wipe-off board along with some communication tools for someone in his condition. He kept trying to tell us something, but it was exceedingly difficult to understand. John kept pointing at pictures to communicate to us what he was trying so hard to say. He ended up writing chicken with his left hand as best he could. Thank God his nurse Gina was exceptionally good at understanding John.

A couple of weeks into John's fall as he was still lying unconscious, we were all still upset and having a real hard time with
what had transpired. The Nurse Practitioner, Ariel, wanted the
ICU to induce a coma because she thought that John's injuries
were so severe, she thought it would be better if John had some
uninterrupted time to heal on the inside. One doctor did not
agree at that time and said no. He said they would see how he
is tomorrow, and then they will decide. The following day came,
and the doctors decided they did not have to do the induced
coma. Thank you, God! The doctors said that when you suffer
a brain injury like John has, then it's a slow, slow process. That
is one of the reasons they could not give us updates on John's
prognosis. The doctors simply did not know to what degree
John's injuries were going to affect his overall condition. It was
much too early. "It simply takes time," Peter in the ICU said.
"Claire, slow and steady wins the race. I know that John has a
severe TBI but just know, Claire, that you are going to have
bumps in the road.and that's normal. It's OK. Just stay slow and
steady. Otherwise, you may try to rush things. We don't want
you to do that. Peter said.""It is really hard," I said. "I have never
been in this position before, where someone I love so much is
on the brink of life or death, suffered a traumatic brain injury
and loss of his entire right side. John is the most important man
in my life and my children's lives aside of God."

The following day was Monday. Boston Medical Center was
admitting more and more patients as the ICU became full. They
needed an ICU bed and felt John was stable enough to go to a

step-down unit even though he was number eight on the list. Nurse Peter said John was the most stable and there was greater hope that he would recover more. The goal was to get John to rehab so that all the hard work of walking, talking, and using his hands would begin. We knew if John could get to rehab, he would give it 110 percent because that's what he did in life. He gave 110 percent in everything he did. He was physically and mentally strong. I repeatedly told the doctors, "You don't know John, but he was as strong as an ox. He gives 110 percent in everything he does. That is who John is." If anyone could make it, it would be John.

After almost three weeks and still unconscious, John was brought to a step-down unit. Every two hours the ICU doctors would come in and try to wake up John just making sure he was not slipping into a coma. Then it was every four hours and then every six hours. The temperature in the room rose to ninety degrees, and I told them that John does not do well in the heat. They wrapped him up in cold packs because his body temperature was spiking up to 104 degrees. They contributed to it, in part, because of how hot the room was, but they did have people in there trying to fix it. John's nurse Valerie, who worked in the step-down unit, was a traveling nurse living in Dorchester. She was so good to John. Valerie said, "We must get him out of this room because I cannot do a proper neurological assessment on him." John's nighttime nurse Pat, from Squantum, tried to find John an empty room on the floor because he wanted to keep an eye on John. They became best buddies. You see, we were from Quincy and Pat was from Squantum, which was a five-minute drive away from our house. Pat also knew a lot of the same people that we knew. Having that camaraderie with each other made us feel more and more comfortable that John was at the right hospital. However, there was no room for him to stay on that floor.

John was moved upstairs to another room, where Grace became John's nurse. She was so nice and a Christian from one of the islands. I told her that John loved Christian music, and Grace started humming to him right away as Britney wrote things down on the white board in his new hospital room. Christian music was on and playing in the room all the time.

Then, suddenly and out of the blue, John started praying to my sister Barbara saying that God doesn't give you more than you can handle! Where the heck did that come from? I am telling you, God answered so many prayers. You are a miracle, John, you really are. Barbara has been an incredible sister and so emotionally supportive to me that I truly do not know what I would have done without her. To make things worse, Robert was there about a week and a half when suddenly he got sick. That was in January, right before we knew about the COVID-19 virus. He had a bad case of what was diagnosed at that time as walking pneumonia. I now had to leave John at Boston Medical Center to bring Robert to Tufts New England Medical Center. Like father, like son—they both had pneumonia. That is when COVID-19 just started breaking out, and we really did not know a lot about the deadly virus just yet.

Robert went to his primary care doctor a couple of times and then to urgent care. He bounced around doctors like a ping pong ball. We wondered along with his doctor about the possibility of Robert having had contracted the COVID-19 virus. I must admit that it was really draining trying to be there for my husband and at the same time trying to take care of our son Robert. What an emotional roller coaster!

God kept giving us hopeful signs every day when his fingers and toes started moving ever so slightly. We were getting off the elevator, and when the doors opened, there was our neighbor Pastor Wayne, who lives right across the street from us. "Hi, what are you doing here, Pastor?" I said, "I am a chaplain here. "Oh, that is wonderful. I thought you might have been here visiting someone," I said. I told Pastor Wayne that we were here with John and explained the situation and what had happened to him. He was incredibly surprised and started to go into his room. He saw that John was sleeping and said he would check back in with John whenever he could.

We also ran into an old friend, Paul, at Boston Medical Center. He used to lead worship at Christ Community Church in Dorchester when my family attended. What a small world. Paul, who was a Berkley graduate, and his wife, Danielle who would often accompany him during Sunday praise and worship service, were good friends of ours. Paul was now an employee and the Associate Director of Operations at Boston Medical Center. He went in to see John almost every day and prayed for him. Thank God for Paul and the faith he and his family have. When it came time to choose what rehab John would be going to, our social worker Lisa, didn't have any answers for us yet. "If Lisa could get John into Spaulding Rehab Hospital in Charlestown, our first choice, that would be wonderful," I said. As we were talking on the phone, Lisa said, "What about Braintree Rehab as a second choice? They are both really good Rehabs and have great reputations." I could not have agreed with her more.

As I was driving into BMC and pulling into the garage, my cell phone rang. I answered it, and It was Lisa. She called and said John was going to Spaulding Rehab Hospital in Charlestown. Another prayer answered by my graceful and amazing God! John is going to the place where seven years ago he wrote a poem for the survivors of the Boston Bombings in 2013. He hand delivered them in person, in a frame printed on paper with the United States flag waving in the background. I remember John and I bringing them to an older female chaplain at that time. I cannot remember her name. Who knew that John would end up at the exact same place where the victims of that terrible and tragic day were? It would be the same place that John hoped to bring a sense of patriotism, love, and comfort to the survivors. Only God knew that Spaulding Rehab Hospital in Charlestown would be the exact place where John was going to start his recovery journey some seven years later. He would reveal His love and glory to John only in the way that He could.

Do not let an act of evil define who you are but instead reach deep, deep down into your soul and begin to bring out the new you.

Let the love of family, friends and from millions of people around the world begin to shape, mold and inspire you especially when despair and discouragement are knocking on your doorstep.

Remember that you are an overcomer and you hold within you the God given ability to move forward through your pain and circumstance and become transformed for a greater reason and for a greater purpose in life.

Don't allow your new normal to be a self defeating deterrent, but instead let your true spirit of courage, determination and perseverance become the catalyst for all of you so that you would become an inspiration and a light to many.

We are all with you and watch with great gratitude your endurance and human spirit. We will stand by you and along side of you as you begin to travel down this new and at times most difficult road with great hope, compassion and resolve.

Our continued prayers and support will remain with each and every one of you and your families.

For all of us Bostonians and from all across this great country of ours and from all around the world, we too are in the process of grieving and healing with you and the families who have lost loved ones.

You will never be alone; we are all in this together.

Stay strong, stay Boston Strong!

A Bostonian

God has fulfilled so many prayers and expectations, far beyond my understanding. God is simply amazing. He really is! I would tell everyone, "When the doctors don't have any answers, God does! When I needed strength, God comforted me and gave me strength I had never known. When I needed support and my hopes were shattered, God placed my family, my church family, and Catherine's family in our lives. What a blessing they all were. When the situation according to the doctors was grim, bleak, and hopeless, God showed us victories every day, which gave us hope. When the doctors didn't have any answers, God did. God was so faithful and knew the desires of my heart, and that was to save John's life because John was the most important man in my life aside of God. Thank you, Jesus!"

WHO AM I

Leaving Boston Medical Center for Spaulding Rehab Hospital in Charlestown, Massachusetts, was another answered prayer. I don't mean it to sound like I'm not grateful to BMC and all the incredible staff and workers there, because I am. In a sense, my family could now breathe a collective sigh of relief as they were all praying hard for me just to pull through. I know, personally, that the power of prayer is more prevalent and stronger than we think. With so many people praying for me, many unknown, I genuinely believe that is the only, and I mean the only, reason I am here today. We look at the move from BMC as a next step in my early recovery journey. In a semi-bewildered state, with severe double vision and coughing associated with Pneumonia, is how I entered from one world-renowned hospital to the next. Then, on top of all that, I would develop a bad respiratory infection.

Once at Spaulding, I was wheeled into a room on the 7th floor with a fabulous view overlooking the park and harbor below. You would have to be crazy to complain about the ocean view and watching the airplanes taking off from Logan

Airport. My wife was faithfully by my side, and I remember Claire putting up pictures on the wall near my footboard. They were photos of life before the accident and what life was like back then. My family and I all together arm in arm in a picture overseeing Lake Winnipesauke in Meredith, New Hampshire. It was nice seeing the whole family all together once again. Putting a picture of my dog Butterball on the wall made me long for home even more. Butterball, our precious twelve-year-old Golden Retriever, would meet me at the door, with her tail wagging, and she always had a sock in her mouth. I miss those days more than you know. We loved camping and going up north whenever we could. As a family, we loved spending time out in the great outdoors, and when we could, we would bring Butterball along with us. We loved going up North to Meredith, New Hampshire, which was especially beautiful during the foliage season.

It was at Spaulding Rehab Hospital in Charlestown where my new normal for the very first time would hit me square in the face. The first night, I remember looking straight up at the ceiling at the Hoyer lift. In case you don't know what a Hoyer lift is, it is an electronic lift operated by one or two persons that attaches to the ceiling and rolls out on a metal channel. Once rolled out, the nurse or nurse aide centers it above the patient and then lowers it down.

You are then strapped in, and it lifts a person up and out of bed who cannot do it for themselves. Then, they lower the patient down into a wheelchair or a gurney depending on whether ambulance transport is needed. Usually, the Hoyer lift is meant for patients who are partially or totally paralyzed. I was on the seventh floor, or brain injury floor, of Spaulding Rehab Hospital and for good reason. Preliminary evaluation of me was a severe TBI, or Traumatic Brain Injury due to the fall. That night is when I first realized that I could not move my entire right side, but I could move my left. It was like nothing ever happened to my left side. I could not move my right arm, leg, or foot, no matter how hard I tried, and believe me, I tried. I remember saying to myself, "Why me, Lord, why me? Why must I be basically and physically useless to my family? I was the trained Union Carpenter since 1986, and I was the one who always fixed up the house and repaired it. I was the one who joint-compounded and sanded all the seams, walls, and ceilings. I was the one who did a lot of the painting and put down the bathroom floor. I was the one who built shelving down in the basement for more storage, and what about my neighbor Barbara's home? She lives diagonally across the street from me, and she is ninety-five years old this past June, Lord. How am I going to help that poor woman? Why me, Lord, Why?"

I was feeling sad and utterly useless. As a husband, father, and human being, I was having the classic pity party for myself. Why did this have to happen to me, Lord? I would ask over and over. After all, I was the one who, as the Bible says, was supposed to be the head of the household. I was the one who was a domesticated man always willing to help to fold laundry, do dishes, mopping, sanding, sweeping, and waxing floors. I was the one that helped discipline the kids when necessary and helped make family decisions. I was the one who was always trying to help my wife so the burden would not fall so heavily on her.

The Bible says that You created woman as a helper. How am I supposed to live up to my side of the bargain? Why me, Lord? Why?

One thing I could never get used to at Spaulding Rehab or comfortable with was going to the bathroom in bed. I truly don't know how anyone could unless they were totally paralyzed with no feeling in their lower body. Feelings of shame and guilt would overwhelm me, and I would curl up in a ball, like a little child, especially when I was pooping. I had no feeling on my entire right side, so I could not just get up and go to the bathroom. Whenever I felt like I had to go, at first, I thought I wasn't quick enough in letting the nurse's aides know by pressing the emergency bell. After all they did have other patients to attend to. I found myself constantly apologizing for going the bathroom in bed simply because I was not used to living like this at all. The staff was so nice to me constantly saying, "John, it's OK. Don't apologize, we see it all the time. It's part of your medical condition. You'll get better as time goes on. I know that it's hard for you now but try not to worry about it so much."

Apart from that, another situation I could never get used to or comfortable with was having a woman wiping my bum. For me, it was one of those personal and individual acts that I was used to doing all by myself. But as time passed on, I came to realize this would all be part of my new normal. If that were not enough, during the early morning hours I would get a sponge bath by staff members, two or three times a week. It was extremely uncomfortable for me having female bathers wash me up. Before the accident and for long as I can remember I was taking showers all by myself.

This was all so strange and foreign to me. I had to learn pretty fast that all this female interaction, at least for the foreseeable future, would be commonplace. Now that I've had about ninety percent of females helping and attending to my every need, I have learned to be profoundly grateful and appreciative of the wonderful women of Spaulding Rehab. To put in its proper perspective, my Physical therapist Dr. Abbey was a woman, my Occupational therapist Alana was a woman, and my Speech therapist Lara, or Red, was a woman. I would say about ninety-five percent of the nurse's aides were all women. My primary nurses were all women, and one of my doctors was a woman. Thank you, Lord, for showing me the importance of just how ignorant I had become toward women. Thank you for lifting the blinders off my heart. One thing that I have experienced firsthand is that You do not make mistakes, Lord God. We do.

At nighttime, just before I was going to bed some of the nurse's aides would offer me the option of putting on a Urine catheter or not. Since I found myself going pee a lot during the night and sometimes making a wet mess, I thought it made a lot of sense. It wasn't the most comfortable thing going on, but it was quite helpful. I must say that it didn't work all the time as it would slip off sometimes when I was sleeping. In a sense, the Catheter gave me a false sense of security. When it did come off, it would cause an awful mess. As soon as I realized what had happened, I would ring the emergency assistance bell. An aide would then come in and do whatever was necessary to clean me up and make me comfortable again. My primary day nurse, Shauna, was not a fan of wearing the Catheter during the day at all. She would say to me, "John, why do you still have the Catheter on?" I said, "It is easier for me, so I don't make a mess. What if I couldn't grab one of your helpers in time?" She understood why I felt that way but looking at the big picture of things like getting me to use the bathroom, Shauna said it wasn't a good idea. "Please try to remember, John," she would say. It took about three or four times because of my brain injury and consequently my memory to remember.

When I was being transported back and forth to Mass General Hospital in Boston for a C.A.T. scan of the brain, I remember one of the ambulance drivers talking to my wife and I. We both thought that he was a genuinely nice and a polite gentleman. He was also a handsome young man, and as best we could tell, he was around Shauna's age. Shauna was a good-looking girl nurse, and it's funny because she said at the time that she didn't have a boyfriend. A short time had passed, and Shauna would ask me questions about him like, what did he look like and what color hair did he have? "I'm trying to remember if I've seen him before," she would say. "I'll have to keep an eye out for him because we see ambulance drivers here all the time." That's all we needed! Claire may be my wife and I the patient, but we were both conspiring together to become matchmakers.

My PT, who I fondly call Dr. Abbey, probably had the most difficult job as far as results go. She was responsible early on for strengthening my leg, quads, and my core. She would constantly get me up out of my wheelchair with the gate belt on and walk me with a quad cane. Dr Abbey was always by my side the whole time. She was always bracing her knee against my right knee so that it would not buckle. If it were not for her assistance, believe me, it would buckle 100 percent of the time. As I look back when we first started, I realize just how important it was to try and strengthen all the muscles in the foot, leg, buttocks, and core. Even though it was exceedingly early on, Dr. Abbey was truly a blessing. Unbeknownst to me, Alana, my Occupational therapist, also had the big picture in mind. After all, I was new to all of this. She told me I was to do bed-to-wheelchair transfers along with toilet transfers. Alana would encourage and help me do them in the bathroom which was part of my room. The room I was in was more like a private room. She would also show me how to use the hand shower, shave, and brush my teeth while washing up at the sink. Since my right arm and right leg would not react to any degree on their own, maybe, just maybe, there might be some hope to grab onto. Alana had just started electrotherapy on me, and that is when I felt my fist glimmer of hope. After feeling and seeing for the first time the movement in my right leg and arm, I got so excited and said, "Lord, why are so good to me?" My "poor is me" attitude or pity party just took a big hit and was becoming a thing of the past.

Learning how to eat, walk, use the bathroom, shower, and wash up all over again at the age of 59 was very disheartening. It was a lot easier to just give up and say to myself, "Whatever happens, happens." That is how much focus I had on myself rather than on my God and those important family members around me. I remember a Pastor preaching one Sunday morning years ago asking everyone to spell out in their own heads the word "sin." So, I did, and then he said, "What's in the middle of it?" I said to myself, the letter "I." That has stuck with me to this day. That sermon that was preached years ago has allowed me to look at myself and my life in a more biblical way. It's helped me immensely get through this most difficult time.

Poor Job in the Old Testament, he had suffered so much. He was stricken with boils all over his body and lost his entire family and all he owned at the hands of Satan. Paul the apostle suffered immensely as he was blinded, shipwrecked, imprisoned, beaten, and left for dead. I have personally researched the horrors of crucifixions and watched the *Passion of the Christ* many times. I am reminded of the unbelievable sufferings of my Lord Jesus Christ. Who am I? I have not been afflicted with boils all over my body or had my entire family killed, as Job did. I haven't been blinded, beaten, left for dead, or imprisoned, as the apostle Paul was. I haven't had nails driven through my hands and feet and was left hanging on a cross for three hours, as my Lord Jesus Christ was. Who am I?

LEAVING SPAULDING

I GENUINELY ENJOYED MY FAMILY COMING BY TO SEE me almost every day at the Charlestown Spaulding Rehab Hospital. Sometimes they would even come back twice a day. I would say to my wife, "Why are you coming to see me twice a day? I am sure they're charging you every time you park in their garage. You're also doubling your driving time and gas mileage coming from Quincy to Charlestown on top of taking care of three kids too!" Don't get me wrong, I was profoundly grateful to see all of my family as much as I did. I truly was. Our financial situation was at best just somewhat stabilizing when I was healthy and up and about. We were the type of family that lived week to week, and I didn't want to put that type of heavy financial burden on my wife.

One thing the accident did not take away, to a large degree, was my memory. I remember telling all three of my kids— Britney, twenty-five, Brianna, nineteen, and Robert, seventeen— that I was terribly sorry for the condition I was in. "I am going to be a better father to all of you, just give me some time," I said. My poor wife Claire and all that she was about to endure and already had because of me was heartbreaking. I just wanted her to know that I was terribly sorry for the condition I was in. "I will get healthier, Claire, and be a better husband. I will not be so busy that I would emotionally neglectful you like I had done in the past." It wasn't like I was a bad husband or father toward my wife and children, it's just that I was pretty down on myself and depression was really setting in. I couldn't help Claire and the kids the way that I was used to.

Here I was, lying in a hospital bed with almost no movement on my entire right side, staring at a Hoyer lift attached to the ceiling. Little did I know that it would be my only way of getting in and out of bed. It would become part of my new normal for the foreseeable future, and that only added to the oncoming depression. I felt totally useless to everyone around me that I loved. I wasn't used to being down for any period of time, never mind the accident. My humanity was just starting to come through and come through boldly.

Ever since he was a child about eight years old, I had been teaching my son Robert baseball. Before the fall Robert helped me put up a fifty-foot batting cage in our back yard. I was very right hand dominant, so I used to pitch to him as a righthanded pitcher always having the net or L-screen in front of me for safety. We would also use the Jugg's pitching machine, which threw curve balls and fast pitches up to ninety mph. We would also go out and practice on many different baseball fields in and around Quincy. I would hit him ground balls and have him throw into a net we had set up at first base. It was a large golf net I had bought off an individual and we weighted it down at its base as we were trying to mimic a first baseman. By attaching a circled target to its center, we were working on Robert's arm strength and accuracy at second base. We even went inside at TJO Sports in Stoughton practicing ground balls and pop-ups. By doing so we were working on Robert's fielding techniques and defense. I even have a video of former great Boston Red Sox catcher Rich Gedman pitching to Robert during the winter classic at the TJO Sports Complex. Regardless of his fame and after talking to Mr. Gedman, I walked away saying to Robert, "What a nice fellow that man is."

The New York Yankees, Detroit Tigers, and San Francisco Scouts and others were also in attendance. They were instructing Robert, as well as all the rest of the young prospective teens. Some of the different states included New York, New Jersey, and Massachusetts. During the spring to fall months we were your typical baseball family, as we would travel to different cities and tournaments. Some of them even had college scouts in attendance. That is the lifestyle that I left behind.

At Spaulding, I would wake up to a new schedule on the whiteboard for me every day. Brian would come in usually after dinner to copy down the new schedule on the board for the following morning. He also helped the physical therapists and whatever they needed. Brian was sort of a swing guy, as we would say in construction. He might have been from Seattle, Washington, and losing the Super Bowl to us, but Brian was genuinely a nice guy. Usually, Alana, the OT, or Lara, the

Speech therapist, would be first up to start my day. Sometimes, Lara would come during breakfast to see how I was swallowing and tolerating certain foods. Sometimes she would come in just after lunch and wheel me down to her office for therapy. I must say hats off to the kitchen staff because the food there was quite good. Every night a woman would come around to take orders for the following day. You would be able to choose from a variety of different foods and desserts for breakfast, lunch, and dinner. It was all based according to your diet, of course, and ability to swallow.

When you suffer a TBI as I did, they would start you out with thickened drinks and some pureed foods, which was the norm. They're really testing your ability to swallow. Everyone's ability is not the same, and they just wanted to make sure that you didn't choke on your food. They use a grading type of system for lack of a better term, and if you are as fortunate as I was, you would graduate to the next level. The grading steps are then signed off by the speech therapist who is trained in a patient's ability to swallow and swallow safely. I was blessed enough to have a wonderful speech therapist who saw me through my early recovery process. Eventually, during my time at Spaulding, Lara would graduate me to basically eating anything I wanted to eat. Now that's what a man likes to hear. Oh, did I mention that she was a redhead too?

It may be hard to understand for some, but a TBI can affect the muscles in your mouth that help you swallow. A vast majority of people do not even think twice about it or even at all. Unfortunately, until you have had it stripped away from you, like I have, you will never understand how blessed you truly are. I never in a million years would have thought that I would be in this position, but I am. One thing for sure that this whole ordeal has taught me is just how intricate and marvelous the human body God created is. This might sound stupid to some, but the other day I thanked my brain for the gifts of movement. Now that I am on the other side of my physicality, with lack of mobility on my entire right side, I realize just how much I had taken my brain and body for granted. Without the brain sending messages to the different muscles or muscle groups, you just won't have mobility. I am no doctor and do not claim to be, but in my case and as I understand it, my brain must try and find a new pathway to reconnect somehow, and it must do all of that while trying to heal. That is the only way for me to get close to the mobility I once had. I am under no fallacy whatsoever, and I know it is going to be a long and arduous road, but I am up for the challenge!

If there ever was a time I could put my finger on and say that's when things began to change or evolve, it was with my O.T. Alana and electrotherapy. I remember one morning she wheeled from my room to the therapy room located to the left and just down the hall. There were other people in there doing their therapy, so we sat and used the padded platform closest to the door. She had with her a little meter with wires and electrodes attached to it. As we began therapy, Alana started to tape the electrodes strategically to my right arm as her training had taught her. I thought just another day in the therapy room, and I will do the best I can for her. Little did I know my life was about to change and change forever.

Alana said to me that I was going to feel some tingling in my right arm and to let her know when it got strong. So, I said, "Sure, no problem." She turned the little box on that had a timer attached to it and began to turn the dial up slowly. I felt the electricity get stronger in my arm, and then suddenly, my right hand moved. Excuse the pun, but I was shocked! I asked her to turn it up. This was truly incredible, I thought! For the very first time I could feel my right hand responding and realized that I was not a lost cause after all. The next time I had OT with Alana, she did the same to my right leg, and I couldn't believe it. My leg moved! Since then, I am forever thankful for Alana for her training and encouragement. I am reminded of the scripture that spoke directly to me that day and my lack of faith in Jesus: "He replied, 26 'You of little faith, why are you so afraid?' Then he got up and rebuked the winds and the waves, and it was completely calm "(Matthew 8:26, NIV).

I was so entrenched in what had just happened to me that I could not see beyond myself or my circumstances. Praise be to God for all that He has done and is going to do. I was at Spaulding for several weeks now, and my physical therapist, Dr. Abbey, had me scheduled to have a boot or AFO made for my right foot. It was to help strengthen it as part of her therapy program. She also signed me up for an assisted walking device, which I thought was cool. It was called a LOKO MATT.

Although it may have been hard to put on, it almost seemed futuristic to me. It also had a computer screen attached to it, and I cannot tell you how hopeful that machine made me feel. After trying it and simulating walking without a quad cane for the very first time, I really felt that there was a lot of hope for me. One day, maybe just one day, I could stand straight up and walk again. What a feeling! If I could have cried, I would have. The LOKO MATT gave me the ability to feel like I could walk again one day despite my condition.

My faith in God grew even stronger as a result. Even though I was not physically whole, I could now focus in on the big picture much like Dr. Abbey had to do. She may not see the fruits of her labor right away, but one day she will. She was to lay down the physical foundation to healing and restoration for my leg and foot and do it in a certain time frame due to insurance restrictions. I am determined to see her again to show her just how important she really was in God's big picture of things. There is healing in His time, not ours. Her job is more than her job to me. They do not teach you this in the study books of today, but relationships and trust go a long way in one's healing and recovery. Thank you, Dr Abbey, for you are blessed, and I will come back to you one day a much different person than once remembered.

My good friends Jeff and Ann Mann had heard what had happened to me and called me to see how I was feeling. I'm sure I did not sound anything like I had the last time we spoke. After hearing what I sounded like post-accident, I am sure they both knew that I was not as physically well as I once was. After we spoke on their concerns about my health, Ann said to me that she was going to order some *Jesus Calling* books. She said, "John, do you know some people or individuals you could pass them out to?" I said, sure. My wife Claire would be the very first one, and there is a whole bunch of people right behind her who are caring for me." I had absolutely no problem passing them out and telling anyone about Jesus and the incredible things He was doing in my life. I had been telling all the nurses and nurses' aides that there is no doubt I was going to get better! Only because of my Lord Jesus Christ and the hope that resides in Him as the great healer and restorer. I will continue to heal, and I will continue to carry that belief with me by my example and my word until the day I take my last breath. Most people would not believe how far I have come given what happened to me. This is my last report from world-renowned Spaulding Rehab Hospital in Charlestown, Dr. Frankel, MD, who is also an Instructor in physical medicine and rehabilitation, at Harvard Medical School. He wrote in his progress notes, "John Broderick a sixty-year-old male with spastic right hemiplegia after brain injury. We discussed his progress to date at some length, especially as he is about to complete physical therapy. I think he has really beaten the odds in how he continues to make steady progress with walking, even a year out from his injury."

My God and my family are way too important to me to let down. So as the G.O.A.T. Tom Brady says, "Let's go!" I believe that God has an incredible story to tell through my healing and

His amazing works in my life. I am truly comforted by what it says in part of the Old Testament in Deuteronomy 31:6 NIV, "He will not leave you nor forsake you."

Near Saint Patrick's Day in March, I received a shopping bag full of *Jesus Calling* books, courtesy of my good friends Ann and Jeff Mann. I gave the first book, which had a beautiful white hard cover, to my wife, Claire. I was in contact with so many people attending to me during the day and night that I felt I had to pick and choose. I thought to myself, "Who would really appreciate the books?" I must admit it was easy, as most of the individuals that I interacted with were believers. So, I gave the books to different nurses and nurses' aides. I even gave one to my doctor, Dr. Young, and he took it graciously.

There was a woman that came around periodically, and she passed out flyers to all the patients on current events happening at Spaulding. I was very intrigued by the speakers they had on one flyer. After showing it to Claire, we thought it would be a good idea that we go and hear what they had to say. So, when the time came, Claire wheeled me out of my room and into the meeting room, where the speakers were to give a talk about their incidents of TBI and the healing that followed. It was crowded when we got there, so Claire wheeled me toward the back of the room. The speakers got up one by one and told their individual stories of recovery from their TBI injuries. I also liked the format because it was a lot like the ones that Claire and I used to run when I was a Celebrate Recovery Christian Ministry leader for many years. We looked at this meeting as a form of support if you will. One of the speakers absolutely floored me when he told the crowd what had happened to him. If you saw all three of these young men, you would have never ever thought any one of them suffered a TBI. All three of them walked, talked, and acted like nothing had ever happened to them. The gentleman that left me in awe was Pedro. He was shot in the head by a drive-by shooter 6 times, and he appeared to be simply fine. I thought it was amazing that he was still here and alive. They had all suffered one form or another of a TBI, as I did.

As the session went on, I remember looking around the room and seeing a woman with blond hair sitting about ten feet from my right. She was with a young girl who I assumed was her daughter. She appeared to be in a nonresponsive state and looked asleep with her head tilted back on her headrest. If I had to guess as to her age, I would say she had to be in her late teens to early twenties. I remember, for some reason, I kept looking back almost staring at times at her and her mother. After it was over, I felt compelled to talk to them and had Claire wheel me over. I introduced myself and said hello to her mother and told her that there was great hope for her daughter. Just give it some time and keep the faith, I said. I then explained what had happened to me coming from zero mobility and given last rights not knowing if I was going to live or die to where I currently was. It was nothing short of a miracle, I said. I told her just give your daughter some time and keep the faith, believing she is going to get better. Just give her some time. I know it was the nudging of the Holy Spirit and what the Lord was doing in my life. I remember I kept looking over to my right toward her and her mom, almost fixated on them. I thought to myself and hearing inside my head, "John, you were once in the same uncertain place. Just look at her and see where you are today, never mind tomorrow. Go tell her mom of the good news and what I am doing in your life." I remember telling her father the same thing. Just give her some time. Now, I don't know why I was drawn to Gail and her daughter, but I was. When the Spirit of God nudges you, as it did me, then go as it leads you. We had a wonderful time talking together. I honestly believe it was to give Gail the hope that her daughter Hannah could and would get better.

As soon as I got clearance from Dr. Abbey to wheel myself around my floor, I was so excited. I had hairline fractures on the outside of the right thumb in two places at that time. At Spaulding, my arm had plopped off the wheelchair one day and hit the wheel area hard, causing the injury. I had been wearing a hand splint for weeks. You could say that is one of the drawbacks of having lack of control or extremely limited mobility on my right side. After it healed, I was off and running. My newfound joy had transformed me into more of a positive person and surprised my family with this new form of exercise. I would call my wife at night to thank her and the kids for loving and being there for me, and then I would tell her how many laps around the floor I did, with a chuckle. Two laps around the entire floor would be commonplace for me.

I got a real big surprise one night when Pastor Mike Feehan and Miss Arlene showed up at Spaulding Rehab to visit me. They are both a blessing from God and longtime friends. I found it especially gratifying that Pastor Mike, while having his hands full as a father, husband, and a new church planter that he would come visit me. He also came in quite frequently, which says a lot about him, Beth, and his family.

You know how some people just stick in your mind sometimes, for whatever reason. That was the case for this young man named Kevin. He was just over six feet tall, a man of color, and wore a thin beard. You could say we hit it off like peanut butter and jelly. Kevin was the sweetest man of color I had ever met, other than my late best friend Jake Coakley. He would come in just to check up on me and to say hello. Kevin was a Christian like Jake and me. At the end of our conversations, we would both be thanking God for all that he was doing in our lives.

Just before we were scheduled to leave Spaulding for a step-down unit, my wife Claire had a great idea on how to thank everyone for taking good care of me. Chocolate-covered Strawberries. Lisa and Christina of PUREFECTIONS chocolates in Quincy Center had the absolute best Belgian chocolate–dipped strawberries around. I thought it was a great idea, so Claire brought me in some. Right away she wanted to give one to Shawna and Kearston, who were my day- and nighttime head nurses. So, we gave both one and deservingly so. They were both so good to me. I ended up giving out all the rest of the chocolate-covered strawberries quickly, so Claire brought in a few more. I had to make sure to give one to Kevin, and they all were very appreciative of our way of saying thank you for what they had done.

I must admit that It was an incredibly sad time for me as I was about to leave Spaulding for another Rehab. I had just spent over five weeks at Spaulding and developed some incredibly special bonds and relationships there. My wife and I were particularly fond of Zara from East Boston, or girlfriend, as we called her. I adopted Cindy and Jennifer as my daughters because they were exceptionally nice to me. I will miss all of them, young and old. There will come a day when I surprise all of them by walking in and saying thank you. My hope is that they would see just how important all of them were to me. That is my goal for my God and my family.

The last day at Spaulding I remember taking what was to be my last lap around the seventh floor. Only a couple of doors down from my room as I was wheeling myself down the home stretch to my room, out of the corner of my right eye, I noticed a blond woman sitting with her daughter. It was Gail and Hannah, the ones I had spoken to at the meeting. As I passed and went by their room, I felt a strong sense of guilt. So, I backed up, knocked on the door frame, and said to Gail, "Excuse me, I'm sorry to bother you. I just wanted you to know that I am leaving in a couple of hours, and I probably won't see you again. I just wanted to say it was a pleasure to speak with the both of you." Hannah was basically in the same condition as I last saw her at the meeting. I said to her mom, "Do not worry, your daughter is going to be fine. Just give her some time. Tell your husband to keep the faith, and just give her some time." I can only explain that there was an internal nudging of the Spirit that made me feel like I just had to go over and give her the hope that resides in Him one more time. I was once there, I kept saying to myself internally, as I kept looking over at her and feeling my heart break for her mom. I did not know Hannah, her mom, Gail, or her father. I never met the family before either. Whenever I get that nudging of the Holy Spirit, I do not ask questions. I just go. Then I give Him thanks.

NEW BRIDGE ON
THE CHARLES

As soon as we pulled into the ambulatory entrance at New Bridge on the Charles Rehab in Dedham, the first thing I noticed was the reddish brick exterior. Coming from Spaulding Rehab Hospital in Charlestown, a small skyscraper type of building made of glass and metal and being closer to the city with a view of Boston harbor, it seemed like a step down. My wife got out of the back of the ambulance, and then they pulled me out and into New Bridge on the Charles Rehab. We rolled in and down the hall, went into the elevators, and up to the second floor. As soon as the elevator doors opened, we were wheeled right over to the front desk for check-in. After they did their paperwork, I was wheeled into my shared room and transferred by a stretcher board into my bed.

After we got settled in and as it was starting to get darker out, I said to my wife, Claire, "You've had a busy day. Why don't you go home?" So, she kissed me good night and said that she would be back tomorrow. I said, "Thank you, Claire and Britney for all you do," and they were on their way home. It was strange at first having a roommate because you could hear everything that was going on and what was being said. My roommate's name was Larry, and he ended up being a good friend to me. I only heard him when he would cry out for help to go to the bathroom. Larry would require lots of help, as he was a one-leg amputee. I've learned personally that Mother Nature does not wait for anybody, and when you have to go, you have to go.

When I woke up the following morning, I noticed that there was no type of lift or Hoyer lift attached to the ceiling like at Spaulding. The only way of getting in and out of bed or going back and forth to the bathroom was by wheelchair or what was called a Sprite. I don't know why it's called a sprite, but it is a handy piece of equipment. The contraption is like a two wheeled dolly for humans that has a standing platform that self closes into a seat on its back side. I found it to be a wonderful option instead of the wheelchair. So, I waited a couple of hours in my room, and then lunch came, and I must say the food there was rather good.

A woman would come by the room to take orders for the next day's breakfast, lunch, and dinner. That would be the norm for food at New Bridge on the Charles. The following morning, I was told I was going to meet my new Physical and Occupational therapists. One thing that really stuck out to me was just how friendly everyone was at New Bridge. It made me feel a little more comfortable interacting with people in a new place because they were so nice. Don't get me wrong, the people at Spaulding were very friendly to me, and we interacted very well together, but New Bridge had a homier feel to it, both inside and out. The rehab facility, where I was being housed, was about three floors high with a view of the parking lot. The view from Spaulding was much more picturesque and beautiful, to say the least.

My new P.T. came in that morning and went over a few things that she wanted to accomplish in Physical therapy. Jessica was a petite girl, probably half my age, bubbly, and newly married. Shortly after, Nicole, my O.T., came in, and she was so sweet and kind. She wanted to go over what she was hoping to accomplish during our O.T. time together. It seemed like it was just one big happy family atmosphere at New Bridge on the Charles.

Coming from Spaulding Rehab, I developed the mentality that I was going to give a 110 percent in every aspect of therapy for my God and family. I wanted to be a better husband and father to my family as I continued to work extremely hard on my road to recovery. How unbelievably good God has been to me allowing me even partial mobility. Coming from the edge of life and death with a diagnosis of zero mobility by doctors and being read my last rights by Father Ignatius has been nothing short of astonishing to me. As I continue to get better and heal from my current condition, I will give my God all the glory! The following morning, my Physical Therapist Jessica came in, and we were off to the PT room, where they had all kinds of therapy equipment. It would be there I was to meet Jessica's helper Haley, or Muscles, as I fondly called her. She was young, energetic, and attending college at Northeastern University to further her career along. I was about 205 lbs. then, and I was not the lightest patient to wheel around. It wasn't that I was heavy or too much overweight, I was just a fairly stocky man before the fall.

A lot of that physical appearance came from bridge building and concrete work. One of those bridges was known as the pinnacle of the central artery project here in Boston named the Lenny Zachim Bridge. I've also done a lot of concrete work building the state-of-the-art Deer Island Sewerage Plant in Winthrop for many years. I was 234lbs. before the fall and had been considered strong and stocky, but some may have considered me to be a little bit fluffy as well. After the fall, I lost about thirty pounds. Either way, Muscles got a good workout pushing me around, and that's kind of how she got her well-deserved nickname. We started our therapy on the hand and foot bicycle machine located in the therapy room. I think it was an early gauge for Jessica to see what I could or could not do. Eventually we would practice transfers to the wheelchair from a padded table platform located in the back of the therapy room. We would eventually graduate to the walkway and handrails, which I really enjoyed.

It was great to be walking again, even though I had limited mobility. During my time with Jessica and muscles, a step platform was added on the walkway. It was another way for Jess to check my balance and muscle strength in my right knee. That had gone pretty well. At first, we did some side-to-side stepping, and then it was time to step onto the platform. It was time to test the knee and see what kind of weight it could sustain. It still was fairly weak and would buckle at times. That went on for a couple of weeks, and I really enjoyed the challenges I faced with the different height steps Jess would put down. April 7, 2020 was the first time I was able to put my right foot up onto the step while transferring all my weight to that leg. Praise the Lord! To me, if there is no challenge to the task, then I feel that anyone can do it. It was the challenge of therapy that drove me physically, always wanting to do better, and that was my mentality moving forward. We would then go in the wheelchair from the therapy room to the hallway to do a little walking. We would also practice wheelchair-to-couch and chair transfers. Jen would use a spot that was designated for visitors and residents alike. That specific area had several chairs and a couch among other décor on it. Jen was another caring and talented woman I interacted with. Unless you've had your balance stripped away from you, as I have, I've got to tell you, doing these seemingly easy and nonchalant transfers is one of the hardest things I have ever done. Having been on your side, having had balance, no double vision, full use of my entire right side including arm and leg, and speaking normally was an absolute blessing. I long for the day of getting back to at least somewhat normal again or whatever God will allow. As I have said before, and I will say it again, I do not accept the condition I'm currently in. I know I can do better, and only by the grace of God I will. I always make sure to tell all my therapists that I am motivated and really want to get better for my

God, my wife, and my children. I would wrap up with Jessica in PT, and we would fist pump each other for a job well done. Then Muscles would push me back to my room as she normally did. Nicole came in shortly thereafter and wheeled me back to the therapy room. The layout of the therapy area consisted of two different spaces. The area at New Bridge that housed the main therapy room, had a walkway with handrails, plenty of big to smaller plastic balls, exercise equipment and a couple of padded platforms or tables in it. The other side we used for Occupational therapy had a hand cycling machine, a set of stairs, Peg boards, more therapy accessories and an adjustable wooden table set up in the middle of the floor. Nicole would then get a nylon material bag and place it on the wooden table for my arm to move around a lot easier. The idea was to make it move with the least amount of friction as possible. We would then practice windmill style movements on the table trying to strengthen the muscles in my right arm. Nicole also had me push my arm straight out, as far as I could, and then bring it back as I sat straight up in my wheelchair, so I wouldn't cheat. It was good therapy for range of motion for my shoulder and shoulder blades.

I remember Nicole was so sweet and took me outside the therapy room to the patio one day. It was nearing the end of our O.T. time together and what a way to close it out. It was a picture-perfect sunny and warm day. We would try picking up small objects to practice opening and closing my right hand. By doing so we were working on supporting the weak muscle strength in my right hand. Tone, to this day, has been a tough issue to overcome. Any time I would yawn, day or night, my right arm and hand would involuntarily fly up, and my fist would clench tightly together. My right leg would follow straightening out so strenuously, it would hurt a little and feel like I pulled a muscle at times. That goes on to this day.

That is kind of what life was like at New Bridge Monday through Friday with Jessica, Nicole, and Haley. The weekends were a little bit different. They were generally scheduled for relaxing from the week's events and therapies. One thing I did notice was that the weekend night staff was not as attentive. Just ask my roommate, Larry. That poor fellow was constantly yelling "HELLO," from his bedside to try and get their attention. Larry had to go to the bathroom, just like anyone else. At times he would wait longer than usual for help and I don't know why that was, but it was. It got to the point I would press my help button any time I would hear Larry say hello, just so they would come quicker. Larry and I became good friends during my time at New Bridge. Claire and my children were always kind and friendly to Larry when they would come to visit. My family was so thoughtful in sprucing up my room with family photos and a picture of family dog. It served as a reminder of what I had to work hard towards before I came home. Flowers and a large balloon in my room was a reminder of just how much my family really loved and cared about me.

My entire family would come from Quincy almost every day. They would even take me out the front entrance of New

Bridge on the Charles, which was nicely decorated outside with tables and chairs. We all thought it would be a welcomed change of scenery and some fresh air. It really was hard being all alone. I don't know what I would have done if it weren't for my family's unconditional love and support.

It was now time for another session with Jessica and Muscles, and off we went to walking in the hallway again. When we first got there, we would make sure the wheelchair was locked on both sides. Then a smaller version of the quad cane was put down just ahead of my left toes. For safety, I would always have my gait belt and arm sling on when walking. Then it was time to stand up! "Make sure you grab the cane and get your bearings," Jess would say. It reminded me of the *Wizard of Oz*. We're off to see the wizard, Jess, Muscles, and John. I felt like the scarecrow saying to myself, "If I only had a brain." Having a TBI, I can say that. We practiced walking with a quad cane, gait belt, and arm sling for a couple of more weeks. I kept pushing myself to walk further than expected, and Jess allowed me too, as long as I wasn't fatigued. Then, one week I had a new physical therapist named Kady who filled in for Jess. Kady was more than up to the task and had a wonderful personality to boot. She was also coupled up with Muscles and they would also wheel me to the hallway to do some walking. Kady too would allow me to walk farther than expected, which boosted my confidence in myself and my God.

After we were done with our physical therapy, I started to hear rumblings of a patient on the floor above us having come down with the COVID-19 virus. The next day I believe it was up to eight individuals that contracted the potentially deadly virus. A woman came in my room the following day, unannounced, and with a mask on. I had no idea who she was, and she said that she wanted to swab both of my nostrils. I said fine, and she proceeded and stuck what looked like a long Q tip way up my nose. She did it on both sides, put it in a vial-shaped tube, and said thank you. It was an uncomfortable test, but it was short. I knew that the test was for the COVID-19 virus, even though I had not been informed. It was that morning I had Kady as my new P.T. We were just about to wrap up our session together when I was told to look to my right. It was Jennifer waving hi and giving the thumbs up sign with a face shield on. Jessica looked to be fully suited up. Nikki, my nurse, was also waving to me with a face shield on to let me know that she was OK too. I can't tell you how relieved I was seeing both of them in person, because during my time there they were such an important part of my life.

It was right then I understood what was happening. The COVID-19 outbreak was spreading at New Bridge on the Charles and was becoming serious. They would have to take every governmental precaution in place to try and protect us all. At that time, we were still learning about the COVID-19 virus and how it spread. Most of the patients were considered compromised just on age alone. I was one of the youngest at fifty-nine but I had type two diabetes and an aneurism in my heart valve. I guess you could say that was enough to put me on the list of compromised patients. New Bridge would eliminate all patient in-house visits, which meant I was not able to see my family in person anymore. I wasn't able to kiss my wife and kids or interact with my family. I can't tell you how much I cherished our time together. I would end up isolating myself to my room and watching world news on TV. I would listen to Quincy's Pastor Aaron Cavin of Life Community Church at night to stay as focused as I could on God's Word. Now I know why God had us cross paths together years prior at Wollaston beach. Pastor Aaron makes the bible come alive and has been blessed with five boys and a wonderful wife.

Wearing a mask outside the room at New Bridge was commonplace for everyone and would become part of my new normal. I would no longer eat dinner at the common table with some of the residents I had wonderful conversations with. Steve, a former little league umpire, was one of those individuals I enjoyed speaking with. We both had a lot in common when it came to baseball. I would tell Steve that my son Robert was on the baseball team at North Quincy High School ever since he was a freshman. He made the senior team roster as a freshman playing up and down the different grade levels under coach Matt Edgerly and staff.

Robert is now going into his senior year at North Quincy High School, and unfortunately COVID-19 has made a mess of his baseball season. Practices and conditioning were all cancelled at the school. It is a shame that they canceled his entire junior season of baseball and ripped an important developmental season away from him. COVID-19 has also cancelled baseball at TJO Sports Complex in Stoughton during the winter months where Robert would practice. It's been truly disheartening to have everything baseball cancelled for Robert or any player's development. I had been teaching and practicing baseball with Robert since he was a little child all the way up to when the fall happened in 2020. I sorely miss and long for practicing baseball with my son more than you know.

Whenever Steve and I got together, we would talk about the time he spent at the little league World Series and his younger days as an umpire. Steve certainly was a talented individual. Other than the staff and therapists, I could no longer have any direct contact with my family or the outside world. Only by cell phone. That was New Bridge's policy. My nasal swab test had just come back, and it was negative Thank God! The last day my wife and kids were able to visit and, as they were leaving, they could hear someone coughing uncontrollably, which worried them and made them extremely nervous. Now that they had tested everyone on our floor, they told us that they decided to move all of us residents to the West wing of the rehab. As a resident of the floor, I really had no idea of what was going on or what they were really planning to do. They didn't share any information with me except that they were going to move us. New Bridge was going to use the entire side I once occupied for COVID-19 patients. The West Wing, where we were being moved to, was adjacent to those infected patients, kind of like a ninety-degree framing square. With me being compromised and so close to COVID-19 patients, Claire the kids and I, were even more nervous. The only type of communication or contact we would have for the foreseeable future would be by cell phone.

Remember we were still just learning about the COVID-19 virus and how it spread. People with underlying conditions and the elderly were dying in large numbers. What the experts were saying was that most of the deaths from COVID-19 were people over sixty-five and in Veteran or Nursing style homes. I fit the underlying conditions part well, having type two diabetes and an aneurism in my heart valve, but fell short of the age description by five years.

Muscles was a big help in cleaning out my drawers and stacking everything I own on a hotel-style dolly. She could have easily worked for a moving company. Off we went just down the hall to my new home in the west wing. When we got there, it was set up pretty much like my old room, except it wasn't a shared one. It was nice to have a single room and with a better view. My new view may not have been of a parking lot, but instead, of an adjacent building with trees leading out to a large open grassy area with walkways. The therapy stayed the same as it was before the move. Kady was my new PT along with Muscles aiding, and Nicole remained my OT.

My day nurse Nikki and Physical Therapist Jessica were now working with COVID-19 patients, and I really feared for their safety. I had seen on TV the stories of police officers and frontline workers that contracted the potentially deadly virus, and sadly some of them didn't make it. Those poor families and what they were going through.

I remember trying to explain on the phone to my wife how to get to the window on the west wing where my new room was so we could at least see each other. My family wanted to come and see me like they did at my former room looking up at the second floor window. That is when COVID-19 precautions were just put in place. Claire and the kids were getting closer as I waited impatiently for them and with great anticipation and excitement. When they were close, Claire said she would call me for walking directions to my new window. Before I knew it, my family was standing below my window outside, emphatically waving hello. They were all so happy to see me in person as I was beaming with excitement and joy. Claire and the kids were so relieved that I wasn't showing any apparent signs of sickness from the COVID-19 virus. They weren't there five minutes when a man came out of the Hebrew Senior Living Complex, which was directly across from me and my window. He reluctantly asked them to leave the premises, as he said my family was trespassing. Even though there were no signs posted across from me that I could see, it was a residence home that was connected to us. My poor family just got booted from seeing their dad and husband, whom they hadn't seen in quite a while. Claire then called me and told me what had happened and that they had to leave the premises right away. I apologized up and down to her for the thirty to forty minute drive they took just to come and see me. My heart sunk and went out to all of them.

That would be the last time I would see my whole family together again at New Bridge. From now on, the only way we would be able to communicate would be by cell phone. It was truly a scary time for all of us. There would be no visual contact with each other, and that alone was heartbreaking. Add to that the spreading of the deadly COVID-19 virus at New Bridge, and we all really became worried. I was now left and felt all alone and secluded to my room except for my therapies.

New Bridge was taking every precaution it could, but that did not mean I was immune to getting COVID-19 at all. Being compromised and near COVID-19 patients only made me, my wife, and family even more worried. I could not catch this deadly virus under any circumstances, or it just would not be good for me. I was scheduled to go home May 1, and with the emergence of COVID-19 and its spread at New Bridge, I couldn't get home fast enough. Claire and I both agreed that for safety reasons only, I would be better served being at home. Don't get me wrong, the therapy was excellent, and the staff there was really good to me. It was just the COVID-19 virus and not knowing for sure how it was spread and infecting individuals that really worried us. It surely didn't help matters that the decision to use my prior wing and the entire floor for infected COVID-19 patients was given the green light. That was overly concerning to all of us, to say the least. As many of the news channels were reporting a lot of the deaths were in nursing homes and senior development homes just like the one, I was in. Don't forget we had a senior development connected to us called Hebrew Life on one side, and we had COVID-19 patients on the other.

I kept praying to God to spare me and my family from this deadly virus. We did not know or weren't told then, but here are the numbers at the Dedham campus where I was as of May 29, 2020, along with the website. The HRC-Dedham campus saw 58 total cases, with 29 deaths. Fifteen of those infected have recovered. (Website: wbznewsradio.iheart.com/content/2020-05-29-hebrew-senior-life-facilities-see-more-than-100-covid-19-deaths.) As I tried to prepare myself mentally for the next step in my recovery, which was outpatient home therapy, I started to get really sad now that I had to go or move on. I would miss everyone, as God once again answered so many prayers from family, friends, and people I didn't even know. I want to thank God for Jessica, Haley, aka Muscles, Nicole, Nikki, Denise, Bonnie, and all the staff of New Bridge on the Charles. I will deeply miss them all. They will be forever thought of by me and my family as an important and integral part of God's plan.

HOMECOMING

It was now time to go home and see my family and my dog Butterball, whom I loved and missed so much. Don't get me wrong, I am very appreciative to all the wonderful people at New Bridge on the Charles, but I certainly felt a lot safer going home. I was scheduled to leave New Bridge on May 1, 2020, but Claire was able to work it out somehow that I could leave on Thursday instead of Friday. She wanted to surprise me with the news, and let me tell you, she did. She pulled up in our silver 2007 Ford Expedition. I got in with her help, of course, and said my final good-byes to New Bridge on the Charles.

We were going to a place where I had not been since January 5, 2020, home. My first ride on the expressway in our SUV with sunglasses on went smoothly. It's always a concern but thank God I didn't get sick with my double vision driving home this time.

Making life easier were friends like the Lawton's and Pastor Mike of New Hope Fellowship Church. They were collectively able to assemble a front entrance handicap ramp free of charge to my family. Members of Pastor Mike's church even brought food to our home when I was hospitalized. What a blessing they have been to my family and me, especially in this time of need.

When we got about a minute from our home, Claire took a left turn off Hancock Street between North Quincy High school and Creedon field. As we were going down Hunt Street, I noticed a purple truck that looked a lot like mine from a distance. Then my wife took a left into the parking lot, and my son Robert hopped out with a big smile on his face. He wanted to show off the truck shining and looking like new. He did a much better job than I ever could. It was a 2007 dark blue Dodge Ram quad cab pickup truck, and I will forever be proud of him for keeping the truck in the condition it was. Robert even trimmed the interior with different color lighting to give it a sense of elegance. I was smiling with appreciation the whole time.

As we pulled up to the front of our house, the fence was covered with welcome home signs and balloons from family and friends. There were even welcome home signs on Barbara's fence diagonally across the street from us. Barbara and Helen were across the street waving hello a sort of welcome home committee if you will.

Barbara is in better physical shape than a lot of people I know. She walks every day, tends her garden, and pulls weeds from her concrete sidewalk. She does her weeding while on her hands and knees. She's just an amazing woman at ninety-five years old. She and her long upstairs tenant Helen had separate but beautiful gardens. Helen has a big beautiful towering sunflower smack in the middle of her yard. As we rolled to the front of the house, I also noticed the pretty tulip flowers that Claire said she and the kids had worked so hard on. Laid out in a circle around our beautiful front yard tree, it accented the yard and the rest of the flowers that lined the fence. It certainly gave our home greater curb appeal and the yard had never looked so good, I said. What a surprise! I was just utterly overwhelmed by all the support of my family and friends when we pulled up to my home. I truly felt loved and appreciated. It felt so good being home with my loved ones and Butterball, my precious twelve-year-old golden retriever.

As I was wheeled up the new ramp and through the front door, there were signs all over the house welcoming me home. There were some from my wife and kids and even one from my dog, Butterball. She was so happy to see me, as her constantly wagging tail gave it away. When I was healthy before the fall, Claire and I had our bedroom up the fifteen stairs and on the second floor of our home. After the fall, everything changed. I could no longer go up the stairs safely to our former bedroom, or any stairs for that matter. My new bedroom would now be located on the first floor. In it was a newly rented hospital bed. It came with a clicker that you pressed the up or down buttons for the head and foot boards to move accordingly. My wife slept on a mattress on the floor right next to me. Claire had a bad back, and it was a struggle for her to put the mattress up and down. She would stand it up on its side during the day and lay it down at night. Putting all the pillows and blankets on top of her mattress was also challenging for her. In the event

I were choking or had an accident during the early morning hours, she wanted to make sure she was there. That was her reasoning, as Claire was always worried about me. All of this was predetermined when I was at the Dedham New Bridge on the Charles rehab.

I must say that my son Robert, who will be celebrating his eighteenth birthday on July 4, has been nothing short of amazing to me. He is known as a firecracker baby by many, simply because of his birth date. He has stepped up in my absence and really helped my wife out more than you know. Robert, along with Claire, even laid down a rug over the old wooden floor to make my new bedroom look even more presentable.

Back from 1986 to 2004 I was a member of Carpenters Local 33, which is the only way my wife and I could afford to purchase our current home. I will always be grateful to Carpenters Local 33, the brotherhood, and the opportunity to provide for my family. I am just amazed at the amount of work that my son Robert was able to get done without me. On top of laying down the rug in the bedroom with Claire, he also took down a fifteen by thirty foot above-ground swimming pool in our back yard. Robert cut up all the metal and stacked it on a trailer to be hauled away. He did this all by himself!

Whenever we needed something, no matter what it was, Bob O'Donnell was always there for my family and I. What a blessing this man has been to us. He even got a trailer to haul all the metal and wood away, so that we would not have to shell out the $450 for a dumpster. He thought it was crazy to spend that amount of money and even delivered the trailer himself! Bob is always willing to help others by putting himself last. That's just the way he is. Bob has always been there for my family and I. I remember first meeting Bob at Beth Israel Hospital in Milton as a male nurse years ago. Every time I see him, I am reminded of the scripture that says in Matthew 20:28 NIV "Just as the Son of Man did not come to be served, but to serve."

Now that we had all the room in the back yard that the swimming pool once occupied, we decided to make a fire pit, since the sand was already in place. From Robert driving us to get all the materials all the way to installation, the fire pit became a family affair. From grading the sand to placement of the circular stones, everyone should be proud of themselves. The way it turned out was truly remarkable. We have already used the fire pit several times and love the s'mores and cooking hot-dogs on a stick. It gave us a sense of camping out in the great outdoors, and Butterball loves rolling around in the sand.

It was the first part of May when, suddenly, we heard a knock on the front door, and it was my new PT right on schedule. She was a small woman and in good shape. If I had to guess, she was a younger, middle-aged woman, with a bubbly personality. Her name was Peggy, and she was just so sweet to Claire and me. After introductions and as the first week went by, Peggy would stretch me out before we went outside to walk or do some exercises. She would also instruct Claire on how to do them properly when she wasn't there. She would then wheel me outside with Claire carrying the cane following and assisting her as needed. The idea was to walk with the assistance of the quad cane to try and strengthen my right leg. We would make sure to have the gait belt and arm sling whenever we would walk, for safety. We chose to walk across the street and on the sidewalk of the Newbury Ave side. It had a long fence in front of the house in the unlikely event I should fall. It was about a straight walk from one end to the other. We would go past the house and then there was a red brick building and eventually to the church parking lot. It was a walking distance of about 140 feet.

There were days that I could walk it with no problems and days I could not. There were times I would need a wheelchair break to continue walking. Following up right behind me was wheelchair Claire, as I called her. Peggy was constantly holding onto my gait belt, as she was trained, so I wouldn't fall. If you do not know what a gait belt is, it's a wide type of belt with loops all around it to help guide and hold onto. It was extremely helpful in the event I should start to lean and potentially fall. It was meant for individuals like me who were unstable on their feet.

Working hard to gain my balance and stability again was no small task. There were times I wondered if that was even possible again. At the end of the 140-foot walk was the church parking lot and front entrance to the newly named church New Hope Fellowship. Peggy saw the concrete walkway that led to the wide stone stairs and said, "Maybe we'll try them in a couple of days. How do you feel about trying them, John?" "I am always up for a challenge," I said. "Sure, let's go!"

Occupational and physical therapy usually would come on alternating days but not always. The next time Peggy would come, she stretched my hamstrings and asked me if I wanted to do the church stairs. So off we went. We rolled down the ramp and out to the fence crossing Newbury Street to the other side. Peggy wheeled me all the way down until we came to the church stairs. I locked both sides of my wheelchair, and Claire, who had been following right behind us carrying the quad cane, put it down on my left side in front of me. When Peggy was in place, as she always was, I would stand up, grab my cane, and get my bearings. Peggy would then grab my gait belt, and it was time to try the stairs for the very first time since I've been home. I tried the stairs at Spaulding months ago for the first time, and I didn't do so well. I remember I had tried them at New Bridge once, and I would say I did OK. Now it was time to take what I had learned from those experiences and apply them to the task at hand. Up with the good foot and down with the bad. That is the way I was taught at Spaulding Rehab and New Bridge in Dedham. Having strong metal handrails on the church entrance steps was awesome. I went up the first step with my good left foot and then lifted my bad right foot. All went well. I went up the remaining four steps the same way and had no problems at all. I got to the top landing and rested a minute as Claire brought up the quad cane. I then walked over to the other side of the stairwell with the cane with no problem and held onto the opposite side metal handrail. I was trying to stabilize myself before attempting the next task at hand. Going down had proven to be much more challenging for me. Down with the bad foot shifting all my weight onto my bad leg and knee was much more difficult. Peggy had my gait belt, and we started. It was much slower than going up. It did not go nearly as smooth as I had hoped it would, but I did it anyway. Now I know what I must work on to get better.

Peggy and Claire were encouraged, and so was I, to a degree. I am always hard on myself, and I honestly believe it's a good thing for me anyway. In a sense, it drives me. I constantly say to myself, "John, you can always do better, and you are never there." There's always room for improvement. Walking up and down the stairs is now incorporated into my weekly exercise routine, weather permitting. Philomena was my home Occupational therapist and really was responsible for my right-side upper extremities and trying to strengthen them for greater mobility. She was also from Quincy, living about five miles away in the pretty Hough's neck section. She was also a truly kind and younger, middle-aged woman, like Peggy, and to our surprise, they both knew each other. They had both worked at Braintree Rehab together in Braintree, Massachusetts, sometime before working with me and after graduating school. As Claire would say, "Philomena really knows her stuff, huh, John?" I agreed. She would also stretch my right arm and shoulder by raising it upward toward the ceiling with the assistance of a cane. I would grasp the cane with both hands as I laid flat on my back in bed and bring the cane up and over my head. One day, she brought with her a hole-and-peg-style board. It was about a one foot by one foot board made of a vinyl Styrofoam-like material. She would then place it on my dining room table and have me try and pull out the pegs from their holes. I couldn't do it without the assistance of my left hand, and after a couple of tries, I was finally able to do it.

Philomena was trying to work on my arm, wrist, and fingers all the while accessing where I was with my right-side shoulder and arm strength. I truly was thankful to God that at least I had some mobility in my right arm, hand, and fingers. Then, my human side would kick in when Philomena left. I would not be happy with myself as far as progress and where I was at that time. Please try and remember I was a Union Carpenter, always expected to perform on the job. Waking up at 5:30 every morning to catch the ferry to the Deer Island Sewerage Plant was challenging. To be in work on time by 7:00 just added to my anxiety. I would carry that mentality through my young adulthood and all the way up to the present.

When I had full use of my body, arms, legs, vision, balance, and speech, I considered myself to be a happy and normal fellow. When I had it all stripped away and had to learn how to walk, talk, balance myself, go to the bathroom, wipe myself with the opposite hand, shower, shave, brush my teeth, get dressed all left-handed and learn how to communicate, it was like being a little baby all over again. It is beyond frustrating for a six-ty-year-old man to learn how to do these things all over again that normally I would have done without much effort. Most people would say, "John, you have absolutely every right to feel that way." It is a lot easier to just give up and fall into a deep depression and accept things just the way they are. It really is. But now, after seeing things more clearly and all the achievements I've been allowed to make, the sky's the limit for me.

I used to struggle mightily with God's timing. It just seemed like He always came at the last minute for me, and I really didn't understand why. Since the fall, I have come to see and understand a whole lot more. My family has been incredible to me, and the amount of love and support has been off the charts. We have never been closer, nor did I know in my heart how much they actually do love me. This may sound crazy to a lot of people, but I am so glad that this fall happened to me. My family and I have never been closer or experienced the love we now have for each other, and I would have never known that living life the way I used to before the fall. I was always so busy and did not realize then what God is showing me now. I wouldn't trade places with anyone in the whole wide world. I thank God, who has taken me from death to life and from zero to partial mobility. With Him in the driver's seat, I know that the best is yet to come.

Philomena would put a rubber ball somewhat deflated down below my feet. She would then say, "John, what I want you to do is bend over in your chair and try to pick up the ball with both hands raising it up slowly. I want to see if you can maintain both hands on the ball while pressing your right hand into it." At first it was difficult, and I would drop the ball, or my right hand would roll off it. After a few tries, I became better at it. Then it was time to use a towel or nylon bag on the table for my right arm. The towel wasn't as slippery as the nylon bag, so we went with the bag. The idea was to imitate zero gravity as best we could or make arm movements as easy as possible. If we didn't have a nylon bag, then we would not be able to see the progress the different muscle groups were making. Even though it may have seemed like slight progress, we would not see the reality of the muscle group's improvement on a harder-to-slide material. We would also practice opening and closing the right hand and stretching the fingers. Right side tone has always been a problem with my body. I call it the invisible enemy because it is unwanted, and you can't see it coming on. It would always come on like gangbusters whenever I would yawn or just get out of bed. My right leg and hamstring would involuntary stiffen straight out and cause muscles to be stretched as far as they possibly could.

The tone would always make my right arm shoot up and clench my fist tighter than a drum. Sometimes I would ask my daughter Britney or Claire, whoever was around, to unclench my fist because it got so tight. Unfortunately, the tone on my entire right side would become an everyday event even to this day. Philomena would then grab some playing cards out of her bag of tricks and hold them out one by one. She wanted to see if I could grab them and close my fingers while holding onto the cards. She was also looking at my releasing ability. She wanted to see if I could spread my fingers apart and drop the cards onto the dining room table beside us.

As far as home Speech therapy went, I had a wonderful woman from Abington. Heather would come by twice a week, and we would work on a bunch of words and blends. We would also work on reading articles aloud, which helped with the pronunciation of words. Otherwise, I would sound like someone who had a lot of bubble gum in their mouth.

As we all know, all good things must come to an end. All home therapy by insurance standards would come to an end in late August or early September. It was now time to look at outpatient facilities nearest our home. After considering several places for the next stage of my recovery journey, I chose Spaulding Rehab Hospital in Charlestown. Having a world-renowned reputation and after experiencing it firsthand, it was a no-brainer. After all it was just after the fall and Boston Medical Center that I was immediately brought to Spaulding to begin my recovery. I chose Spaulding Rehab Hospital because it was there that I realized my God has always been there for me, and it took the fall to make me realize. I truly am thankful to Him for His love, mercy, and His grace.

RETURN TO SPAULDING

IN A SENSE IT WAS SORT OF A HOMECOMING, AS I FELT a special bond to Spaulding Rehab in Charlestown. I know I can't visit my former O.T. or P.T. because of the COVID-19 restrictions Spaulding currently has in place. But one day soon I will see them again, and they will see a newer and improved version of John that they never seen before. I will finally be able to say to them in person, sincerely, thank you.

We were able to get Physical therapy, Occupational therapy, and Speech therapy scheduled for twice a week for outpatient therapy. The second week we were at Spaulding for Speech therapy, I saw Laura, or Red, as I fondly called her in passing. She was my original Speech therapist, and it was really good to see her again and re-establish the bond we once had.

My new Physical therapist was a genuinely nice and polite woman. She is a runner and hiker, which speaks volumes as to why she is in such good shape. Her name is Elise. She is always pushing me to do better, within constraints, of course. She tested me for walking on my own with the quad cane just to see what I could do. Elise would then test me for walking speed with the sounds of beats on her cell phone and eventually for endurance as well. I liked that because I had an audible sound to guide me through, and I did pretty well. She also used the Bioness an electronic device on my weak right knee. In case you may not know what a Bioness is, it is a device that uses electro stimulation to shock or wake up a muscle or muscle groups that barely react on their own. It is controlled on an iPad and can be set to stimulate when you want it. In my case, she would wrap it around my knee velcroing it together, then program it to shock or stimulate my right knee while I was walking in step.

Elise wasn't there one week, and Dan filled in for her. He laid out what looked like a flat plastic ladder on the floor. He had me practice stepping in between the rungs a couple of times. At first it was hard for me, but I am always up for a challenge in therapy. Dan would also have me walking to strengthen my right leg, knee, and quad muscles. The next time I saw Elise, as she had mentioned, we were going to attempt the stairs. They were not the typical set of three or four wooden stairs with handrails I had seen when I was first at Spaulding or at New Bridge on the Charles. Instead, they were right behind the exit door of the therapy room. She wheeled me through with the alarm going off and Claire right behind us carrying the quad cane. Then, I looked up at the stairs. An extraordinarily strong and unsettling feeling came over me. It reminded me of the stairwell I had fallen from. I am all about conquering your fears or facing your demons, but I must admit, at first, I felt very hesitant and unsure. I truly contemplated, can I do this? Then I thought of God and how good, merciful, and kind He has been to me. Then, suddenly, I stood up, grabbed the left handrail, and went straight up the fourteen or so concrete steps with no problems.

Elise said to me afterward I climbed those stairs like a champ. Please don't forget that it was the very first time since my fall I would look up at any stairwell I was going to attempt to climb. Claire put down the quad cane, so I could walk the platform at the top to the other side. Walking to the other side was no problem at all either.

Now I was looking straight down the stairwell. With my internal focus on Him and Him alone. I was now able to look down the stairs and not be afraid of falling. Every rehab taught me that going downstairs was first down with the bad leg. Elise showed me how she wanted me to proceed going down. So, I started with the bad leg going down first, which forced me to transfer all my weight onto it, and then I brought down my left leg. It went smoothly for about the first two steps, and then my right leg began drifting farther and farther toward my left. That is when Elise stopped me and explained that she wanted me to plant my right foot out wider for greater stability and balance. Even though I really tried, I wasn't much more successful. Now at least we know what I had to work harder on to strengthen and control my right knee for our next time together in Physical therapy. There just isn't enough control of my right leg, yet. Elise made sure I got in my wheelchair safely and wheeled me back inside the therapy room. She said, "Good job, John," and off Claire and I went to the waiting area to wait for our next appointment.

We didn't wait very long when my new Occupational therapist Jennifer came over waving hello from a distance for our next appointment. So, Claire wheeled me down and Jen asked me how I felt, and I said fine. She asked if I was experiencing any pain. I said no. She would then bring me to one of several wooden adjustable tables to stretch my fingers, wrist, and hand.

One of the first OT tests Jen had me perform was to take wooden pegs on a small board out of their holes with my right hand. Then I would try to put them back in. I have been diagnosed with neuroplasticity. She knew right away that I had a real problem with tone. Tone is an awful thing to wake up to every single day. Putting the pegs back in their holes seemed almost impossible with my right hand alone. There simply was no control of my right arm and hand, so I could aide it with my left she said. It was still rather difficult, but I was able to accomplish some of it, although slowly. Jen would also lay me on my back on one of the padded tables that wasn't being used to stretch out my right shoulder. She put what looked like a four foot weighted stick in my hands and had me hold it with one hand on each end. She then told me to raise it straight up toward the ceiling like a bench press and hold it for about five seconds and bring it down slowly and controlled. That had gone well. Part of the reason it went well was the practicing I do at home every night in bed with a cane. I originally was taught that by Philomena, my prior home O.T. She even gave me two handles connected by a rope on a spindle to hang on the top of the door frame in my bedroom. It's a great tool to have to loosen up my right shoulder, and it's still there to this day. I am able for the first time since the fall to barely touch my nose with my right hand. It is all God's timing, not mine.

Jen would also have me walk from the wheelchair to the padded tables, which also helped with practicing my transfers. Jennifer is particularly good at her craft, just ask Claire. She is also a unique and pretty-looking woman being Japanese and Irish. One Monday, I was scheduled with Dan instead of Elise because of a scheduling conflict. I've had Dan before, and I enjoyed his pushing style always trying to get the best of my abilities. This time we were off to the concrete stairs, which were through the exit sign and into the back hallway. The alarm would go off all the time, and it took a little getting used to that loud sound. What Dan planned to work on was to strengthen my hamstrings and glute muscles. He had me wheel up to the left handrail in the hallway looking up the stairwell. Up with the good leg and bring up the bad or right. Then he would have me do the opposite coming down. I would start by bringing down the weak or bad leg first. Dan showed me how to straighten it out all the way and then transfer all my 208 pounds onto my weak leg.

"Hold it there," Dan would say, Then bring down the left." We would repeat that ten times. He would then have me walk to the other side, hold onto the handrail, and we would practice side-to-side stepping on the first step only. Up with the good leg first and then bring up the bad, or right foot. Then down with the bad, transferring all my weight on it, and bring down the left.

We practiced that five times each. Dan then had me walk from the stairs through the door setting off the buzzer again and walk with the quad cane all the way to the walkway with handrails.

I must say for a man who was used to lifting heavy lumber and plywood, I was pretty winded. Being strong and stocky doesn't matter anymore. Even the simple things like taking steps, lifting bars, and walking are all a concerted effort for me. I can't tell you how much that affects me mentally at times. It's very disheartening being a sixty-year-old man and learning how to do the things I once did effortlessly and having to do them all over again. When I let my humanity get the best of me, and believe me there are times when it does, I immediately turn to my faith and ask God for forgiveness and for continued strength to help me fight through. This has been by far the hardest thing for me to deal with, and I have dealt with a ton of stuff in my life.

Dan got me up to the walkway and told me to grab the left handrail and then walk up a few steps and stop. He then had me face the beautiful large picture windows in the therapy room by taking a few additional turning-style steps. He then placed a wooden platform that was about five inches tall just a little shorter than the concrete stairs. Dan showed me that he wanted to strengthen my leg by starting with my bad leg raising it onto the platform. So, I raised my bad right leg up placed it on the platform and tried to bring up my left or good leg putting all the weight and pressure on my right leg. It was not easy, but I managed to do it. There were times I was letting my right hip lean out a bit because I wasn't standing straight up. Dan would stop me as the trained professional he is and say I was favoring my left side. It was considered normal given the injury I had, but it had to be corrected hopefully over time. Dan would point that out to me and now that I knew, I would try to stand straight and tall. We practiced that five times before I became like Gumby. Our session ended, and Dan said, "As always, good job, John." I said thank you.

After our session was over with Dan, we went to assisted technology referred by Rick, my Speech therapist. Although all my therapists were on the second floor, assisted technology was located down on the first. It was there I was able to introduce myself to Michelle, who was speaking with my wife Claire back when I was unconscious at Boston Medical Center. You could say Michelle saw me at my worse early on. That is the way we would enter from the garage and take the elevator up to the first floor. There everyone is required to go and change their masks and sanitize their hands due to the COVID-19 virus.

> We were at Spaulding Rehab so much, we became good friends with the front receptionist, Margaret. She is such a pleasant woman and has been very friendly to the both of us. Margaret's been a real blessing to Claire and I. It has been almost a month and time for a progress review test by Elise, my PT. Endurance-wise I scored thirteen percent, better than last month. I was able to walk with a smaller version of the quad

cane for a period of ten minutes compared to six minutes last test. Even though I have had Elise help and stand by me with a gait belt on or a one-person assist, that's progress. I thank God first and then my wife and children for walking me inside and outside of our home and around the new park just blocks away. The extra work is starting to show the fruits of our labor. It's a total team effort, and I wouldn't be able to progress without everyone involved. To all the staff at Spaulding, Dr. Abbey, Alana, Elise, Dan, Rick, Ashley, Michelle, Elise, and Jennifer, thank you! To Peggy, Philomena, and Heather my outpatient home therapy girls, thank you. To Jessica, Nicole, Kady, Heather aka Muscles, Jen, Denise, and all the staff at New Bridge on the Charles. Thank you all. We are all on the same team, as God surely knows. How fitting that I finish writing this book the day my mother-in-law Barbara Hewitt Sr. is lying at the Beth Israel Hospital in Boston. According to doctors, Nanny is going to go home to be with the Lord in just a few short hours. Thank God for His Grace!

REFLECTION

"Therefore, humble yourselves under the mighty hand of God, that He may exalt you at the proper time," 1 Peter 5:6

WHENEVER I LOOK BACK AT MY LIFE AND BEGIN TO think of all the incidents that happened to me one by one, or singularly, I don't think twice about them. I thought, yeah, it was unfortunate, but things happen to people all the time. That's life, and life goes on. Any type of spiritually or divine intervention was not even a thought back then. As a young child, I was taught that my God was a punishing God. I can remember late mom saying to me, "Johnny, God is going to get you for that." My mother was born in Rome, Italy, which is the city of Catholicism and home to the Vatican. Hearing it come out of her mouth especially at that time carried a lot of weight to all four of us young children.

On January 5, 2020, I was rushed to Boston Medical Center, a world-renowned hospital, and Trauma Center. After falling down fourteen stairs, suffering a brain bleed, severe head trauma and developing pneumonia, things did not look good. Whenever the doctors would say to my wife, "We don't know if he's going to make it but expect the worse and hope for the best so when the good comes, if it comes, you'll be happy." As upsetting as that was to hear, Claire responded to the doctors by saying, "Do whatever you have to do to save this man's life. He is the most important man in my life and my children's life aside from God.

It wasn't until I was moved from Boston Medical Center to Spaulding Rehab Hospital in Charlestown that I felt the presence of God come into my life. I specifically remember Alana and Dr. Abbey administering electrotherapy on me and feeling parts of my right side move that I thought would never move again. I went from down and depressed to totally elated! I honestly thought I would never have mobility or even partial mobility on my right side ever again. My faith just took a huge leap forward. Ever since then, with God as my guide, I have never looked back and given 110 percent to all my therapists and in all my therapies. Even though I am currently typing my entire story with one finger on my left hand and one eye closed, severe double vision, four fractured ribs, and confined to a wheelchair with some speech impediments, I am praying for continued healing and restoration from God. I am compelled to write in my current condition by the Spirit of the Lord to show to all the progress He has allowed me to make to date. As I experience even further healing, my prayer is that you will be encouraged and edified and God would get all the glory! Thank you, Lord Jesus!

Now that He has allowed me to see all the incidents collectively over the years, rather than one by one, the blinders are off! I can see clearly and without a doubt that God had His hand upon me even when I was younger. During those most difficult times, when I lost my sister and then my mother, within seven weeks of each other, I thought He wasn't there. He was. I am reminded of what is said in the classic poem "Footprints in the Sand": "When you saw only one set of footprints in the sand that is when I carried you." From almost freezing to death at Pleasure Bay beach in South Boston, having a gun put to my right temple and pulling the trigger, to almost falling forty feet down to an adjacent expressway due to an accident, after drowning in a lake in New Hampshire, and then being pulled to shore to a waiting ambulance, after driving a Volkswagens van and it blowing up on me and burning to the ground, after falling down fourteen stairs suffering a life-threatening brain bleed along with severe head trauma, God is good and faithful all the time! His works for me and His plans to bring Himself Glory are not finished, and neither am I. I consider myself to be nothing more than a grain of sand on the beach, and that is all I truly am. My sincere prayer and hope is that you would be encouraged and lifted up by what God has and is doing in my life. I pray that you would become a beacon of light in this dark and fallen world. I pray whether you're in church or alone, male or female, young or old, that through you His kingdom will be furthered here on Earth. Jesus has been so good to me. May He, His Father, and the Holy Spirit be glorified through these real-life examples and these writings. Everything that God has done for me can only be wrapped up in one special word, GRACE.

Love,
John Broderick

FINDING PURPOSE

SOME PEOPLE SPEND AN ENTIRE LIFETIME WITHOUT finding a reason or purpose for their lives here on Earth. I must admit that when my fall occurred in January of 2020, I really felt that life as I had once known it was over. When I came out of unconsciousness after three weeks at Boston Medical Center, I was trying to process what had just happened to me. I was moved from Boston Medical Center to Spaulding Rehabilitation Hospital in Charlestown feeling totally down, depressed, and dejected. I have never heard of a Hoyer lift before or even knew what it was. Realizing the seriousness of my injury at Spaulding Rehab was only possible because of it. I had suffered severe head trauma and a traumatic brain injury. I just could not wrap my head around it all at that time. Due to a total lack of mobility on my predominant right side, I could not get myself out of bed without the Hoyer lift. The nurse or nurse's aides would strap me in, lift me straight up and out of bed and then lower me down into my wheelchair, like patients who are partially or totally paralyzed.

I had so much going on for me physically before the fall, and I could do just about anything anyone else could do. My son Robert and I built a fifty-foot batting cage in my backyard. He was a particularly good player for North Quincy High School baseball, and he was fast. We would practice his hitting all the time and go to different ball fields in and around Quincy. I would hit him ground balls, line drives, and pop-ups trying to improve on Roberts's defense. On top of baseball, I would use my skills as a Union Carpenter climbing up and down ladders and doing whatever it took to complete someone's construction project. For lack of a better term, I was as normal as anyone else.

Then came the fall. My life and my family member's lives would be severely shaken and turned upside down. I had to learn all over again how to talk, eat, use the bathroom with the help of my wife, wipe myself, wash my hands, brush my teeth, use mouthwash, shave, take a shower in a chair also with the help of my wife, try to get dressed, and do all of that with my left or opposite hand. I was no spring chicken at the tender age of fifty-nine either. Never mind waking up every day with severe double vision affecting my sight and balance and just about everything I did.

Before the fall I had hernia operations on the right side of my groin with doctors implanting a four by six piece of plastic mesh. Shortly after that surgery, I had an operation on the left side of my groin with a four by six piece of mesh being implanted as well. I then had an operation on my stomach and was told that I would wake up with a small one-inch scar. Instead, I woke up with a one and a half foot scar from my belly button up to my breastplate. Doctors would also implant a six by ten piece of plastic mesh in my belly. They said they had to sew my stomach muscles back together again as they were stretched too far apart. The doctors were trying to explain the reason for the length of my new Frankenstein scar. I also had an operation on my right shoulder, as doctors inserted two pins, shaved my bicep, and sewed up the muscle due to right rotator cuff surgery. When I was a young boy, I lived on base in Norfolk Virginia along with many other military families. One day, as I was trying to fit in with all the other Naval housing kids, I was dared to smash a coke bottle on a sewer cover. Being young and impressionable, I took the hammer, and I did. That would lead to my first operation removing a two-inch piece of coke bottle glass that penetrated and stuck out of the center of my left eye. The doctors from the Norfolk Naval Hospital were pleasantly surprised that I was even able to see although a section of my left cornea was missing. You might look a little blurry when I am covering my right eye but it sure beats being totally blind on my left side.

On top of all that, everything that you have read up to this point, my God knows as truth. I have always been the type of man to learn the hard way for whatever reason. I did not realize how Graceful and Merciful God had been to me until the fall. Now that He has allowed me to look back at my life collectively, I can see clearly that His hand was upon me. I have never been as close to my wife and children as I am now, and I would have never known that before the accident. I now know what true love is and the way that God intended it to be. I would not trade places with anyone in the world, even as handicapped as I currently am.

I assure you that I am working extremely hard to overcome this journey of hardship, and with His guidance I will. I do not believe that God is done with me nor am I done Glorifying Him. In the chapter "LEAVING SPAULDING," the girl who was confined to a wheelchair and totally unconscious, Hannah, is the one I felt compelled by the Spirit of the Lord to wheel myself over and tell her mom that she was going to be just fine. She appeared to be worse off than me! Give her some time and keep the faith. Just give her some time, I said to her mom Gail. Hannah is now up walking and talking! I am thankful to almighty God for His miraculous hand upon her as she continues to heal. I just watched a video of Hannah rowing with her brother for the first time in ten months! Glory be to God! With the unconditional love of my precious wife Claire, my two beautiful girls, Britney and Brianna, and my son, Robert, the sky truly is the limit for my healing and restoration. What a blessing to have the timely support of our church and friends along with the limitless prayers of all. I have finally found my purpose: to glorify God, His son my Lord Jesus Christ, and the Holy Spirit. I pray that you would be encouraged and edified by these real-life examples of God's Grace.

"When the peace of Christ rules in our hearts, thankfulness overflows. Even in the darkest of times, we can praise God for his love, his sovereignty, and his promise to be near us when we call" (Psalm 145:18).

Love,
John Broderick